BISON
BOOKS

The Genteel Tradition

Nine Essays by George Santayana

Edited and with an introductory by
Douglas L. Wilson

*Introduction to the Bison Books Edition by
Robert Dawidoff*

UNIVERSITY OF NEBRASKA PRESS

LINCOLN AND LONDON

© 1967 by the President and Fellows of Harvard College
Reprinted by arrangement with Harvard University Press
Introduction to the Bison Books Edition © 1998 by the University of
Nebraska Press
All rights reserved
Manufactured in the United States of America

⊗ The paper in this book meets the minimum requirements of
American National Standard for Information Sciences—Permanence
of Paper for Printed Library Materials, ANSI Z39.48-1984.

First Bison Books printing: 1998

Library of Congress Cataloging-in-Publication Data
Santayana, George, 1863–1952.
The genteel tradition: nine essays / by George Santayana; edited and
with an introductory by Douglas L. Wilson; introduction to the
Bison Books edition by Robert Dawidoff.
p. cm.
Originally published: Cambridge, Mass.: Harvard University Press,
1967.
"Bison books."
Contents: Young Sammy's first wild oats—The genteel tradition in
American philosophy—Shakespeare: made in America—Genteel
American poetry—The moral background—Philosophical opinion in
America—Materialism and idealism in America—Marginal notes on
civilization in the United States—The genteel tradition at bay.
Includes bibliographical references and index.
ISBN 0-8032-9251-1 (pbk.: alk. paper)
1. United States—Civilization—20th century.   2. National charac-
teristics, American.   I. Wilson, David L.   II. Title.
E169.1.S254   1998
973—dc21
97-51357   CIP

Reprinted from the original 1967 edition by Harvard University
Press, Cambridge.

To Mae and Charles Wilson

Introduction to the Bison Books Edition
Robert Dawidoff

This republication of *The Genteel Tradition: Nine Essays by George Santayana*, originally edited by Douglas L. Wilson and published in 1967, is welcome indeed. The passing of time has not diminished the power of Santayana's influential, perceptive, and elegant essays. It is hard to think of any Americanist writings more likely to reward and surprise the contemporary reader. Like his contemporary and antagonist John Dewey, Santayana has suffered the ironic fate of philosophers whose own writings have been obscured by their having been assimilated and in many respects distorted by several generations of readers.

Dewey's writings and his work in the world generated an educationist establishment that guaranteed him a certain readership. But George Santayana's reputation had no institutional coupons to clip. Dewey defined a climate of opinion and a vast program of reform and action. Santayana's understanding of the American cultural climate depended on his view that the philosophic and aesthetic were ends in themselves, alternatives to the kind of action so central to William James, Dewey, and their associates. It was not only that he, like many others, doubted the prudence or efficacy of the pragmatist Progressive program. He did not share the noble hopes that inspired it. He did not believe in democracy. Even Alexis de Tocqueville believed that democracy's inevitability might have positive results. His *Democracy in America* is finally a democratic book. Its strictures on democratic and American civilization have proven congenial to generations of Americans and founded a critique of democracy that has thrived within it. Tocqueville remains the virtual patron saint of American self-understanding and boasts the website and souvenirs to prove it, theme park no doubt to come.

We are probably safe from a Santayana website—by which I mean not Internet access to the writings or scholarship but the honor and horror of commodification. Santayana stands as he stood, pretty much alone. Jefferson, Tocqueville, Dewey, et al. taught Americans what to say. People talk Deweyspeak without even knowing it. Santayana's pithy, clever, and profound remarks, like Groucho Marx's, are his passport to familiarity—you can't speak like either, you must quote their remarks. Even educated people nowadays probably recognize Santayana, if at all, as the guy who thought up that thing about how if you don't study history, you'll repeat it, which seems to suggest watching Ken Burns documentaries or pursuing reincarnation. You can quote Santayana, but you can't use him. The figures who have claimed Santayana have been notably literary in their interests and anything but programmatically liberal or conservative in their views.

The politics of Edmund Wilson, Lionel Trilling, and Robert Lowell, to take three, do not fit conventional Jeffersonian liberal or Tocquevillian conservative ideals or strategies with respect to democracy. Their ventures into the political privileged the aesthetic and philosophic, not as points of view from which to criticize and reform the culture but as standards, superior to the political—*superior*, not irrelevant. Santayana's understanding of the genteel tradition depended on discerning the difference between moralistic reform and moral seriousness. Such a distinction amounts to a point of view outside the terms of American democratic civilization and the discourses it has generated. It is as little patriotic as it is reformist, because it conceives of the life of the mind as inevitably corrupted by worldly attachments. The value and caution in Santayana's writings lie in their singular disdain for the pieties, ideals, and attachments that have characterized American cultural self-understanding. The philosopher in this view can never substitute allegiance of any kind for independence of thought. He did not equate freedom of expression with independent thinking, as we are likely to do. No wonder Santayana's writings have been eclipsed. We can now see how the original publication of this volume in 1967 unintentionally put a period at the end of the long Santayanan sentence in American letters. That hectic time might have profited from Santayana's observer's detachment but, of course, was almost defined by its inattention to everything that mattered to him. The sixties canonized the preoccupation with the present that has led to the marginalizing of the past, which may be the watermark of our own day.

Perhaps we are readier to reconsider Santayana, especially, but not exclusively, his Americanist writings. The years have not dulled his insights because they never dissolved in the Americanist fluidity. His writings might prove a revelation in a time when theory has replaced philosophy, the academic has replaced the scholarly, professionalism has replaced learning, and plants rather than people are cultivated. Beauty and clarity of expression are not thought to have much to do with other than personal truth nowadays. They are suspect pleasures at best. Santayana's detachment might suggest to all parties to the culture wars that the intellectual and literary inheritance of the past is interesting and important exactly because it challenges the orthodoxies and expectations of the moment. Vain hope— and contrary to the admonitory essence of Santayana's essays. If the genteel tradition essays tell us anything, they tell us to beware confusing contemplation with action. If America tells itself anything, it is that anything worth contemplating must lead to action.

It is worth reminding ourselves what the genteel tradition was, since the drama of these essays is in part Santayana's naming and exploring a dominant tradition of American middle-class culture. In our time the shocking has become the very stuff of the genteel, with the argument for the public importance of art frequently advocating what is called the transgressive as the ordinary test of First Amendment rights. At first glance, it would seem that such notions are the opposite of the genteel, since the substantive point of the genteel was to restrain candor, sexuality, and the transgressive. Yet, Santayana saw at the core of the genteel an ambition to reconcile the popular and the high cultural in terms that favored the cultural power of the genteel classes and institutions. He would have been amused but unsurprised by the evidence that the genteel ended up endorsing free-speech relativism, obscenity, and antisocial behavior (and many other things) in its helpless pursuit of cultural control through misapplied moralizing. Genteel tradition referred to the habits of educated, middle- and upper-class Americans who came to substitute art and learning for the stringent moral vision of American Protestantism. Santayana noted that New England, which still influenced American culture, had lost its once savage faith and sense of sin without losing the moralizing habit. The genteel tradition replaced a reformed Puritanism that had replaced piety with moralism and a God-centered vision with one oriented toward the requirements of human community. Literature, art, and philosophy, the humanist and human arts, replaced morality at the core of the New England creed. But the aesthetic was expected to be moral and moral meant decent. Art was not supposed to challenge the orthodoxies and especially the conventions of the society but to decorate fortunate individuals within it. The gentility of the genteel tradition was its false view that art and learning should have a natural connection to the morally sound.

Santayana knew that good books never could be counted upon to make good men. But the genteel tradition insisted on exactly that. Attempts to enforce it blinded the genteel traditionalists to what was really beautiful and true about Americans. In Santayana's view, it was the philistine material and athletic vitality that offended gentility that was interesting about America, its non-art. It is hard for us to recover that climate of opinion. In that time, the genteel tradition was very likely to enact the kind of prudery and censorship we now associate with the conservative religious reaction, such as the attack on the NEA in the name of traditional values. But it was the genteel that censored Whitman, sanitized Mark Twain, anathematized the sexual, and ended up equating art with the parlor and the parlor with the academic. The genteel tradition nowadays can be found in the pale, obligatory defense of publicly supported art on First Amendment and political grounds. But the moralizing habit and the attempt to claim the arts and learning for "moral" purposes is what Santayana meant by the genteel tradition. The best place to find the genteel in our time is probably in the mirror, since the people most likely to be rereading Santayana are we who resemble the genteel traditionalists of his time in our purposes and relation to the culture at large.

Three decades ago, Douglas Wilson could assume a familiarity with Santayana that no longer seems prudent. His valuable introduction tells the story of these essays and their reception admirably, but it is probably a good idea to tell a little more of Santayana's story, especially since certain things are now out of the closet. George Santayana (1863–1952) was born in Spain to Spanish parents, who were also steeped in the middle echelons of Spanish imperial life in the Philippines. Santayana's mother was the widow of a Boston scion of the Anglo–New England merchant-prince Sturgis connection. She left the five-year-old George with his father in Spain to return to Boston to raise his three Sturgis siblings. At age nine, George joined her. There he was educated in the best Boston manner and experienced what was to be his lifelong position as an insider outsider, welcome by virtue of his birth and his talents within the precincts of societies to which he could never feel that he belonged by right. His salad days came as an undergraduate at Harvard, where he drew, wrote poetry, discovered the study of philosophy, made warm friendships, and settled on the tone he was to take throughout his life. He stayed on to study with William James, Josiah Royce, and others in that golden age of American academic philosophizing.

Santayana distinguished himself in his studies and, in his attitude toward them, from his teachers. He sounded a characteristic note of joyous disdain for ordinary philosophical practice early on. He rose to the rank of professor and acquired a following of his own. The confidential report of the redoubtable, modernizing President Charles Eliot of Harvard concerning Santayana's promotion to assistant professor in 1897 suggests the problem Santayana posed to his conventional fellows, a problem he himself understood as a challenge, and the one he still poses to his American readers. Eliot wrote,

The withdrawn, contemplative man who takes no part in the everyday work of the institution, or of the world, seems to me a person of very uncertain value. He does not dig ditches, or lay bricks, or write schoolbooks, his product is not of the ordinary, useful, though humble kind. What will it be? It may be something of the highest utility, but, on the other hand, it may be something futile, or even harmful because unnatural and untimely.

Harvard came to value Santayana, but his career was marked by those key terms "unnatural and untimely" and the further worry about his usefulness. At forty-eight, having come into an inheritance, Santayana resigned his professorship and left America, spending the second half of his life wandering in Europe, where he ended up living in his famous refuge with the Blue Nuns in Rome.

Santayana wrote poetry up to the point when, as he said, his muse deserted him. One senses that it was his candor that deserted his muse. He wrote several philosophical inquiries, works of literary criticism, and books on the history of philosophy. He developed, and in his view perfected, a philosophical system in several big books, written over many years. He was also, memorably, an essayist, whose observations about America (*Character and Opinion in the United States* and "The Genteel Tradition in American Philosophy"), Germany (*Egotism in German Philosophy*), and England (*Soliloquies in England*) are classics of their kind. He even had an American literary success in the late thirties with his novel *The Last Puritan* and finally became, with *Persons and Places*, one of the century's most interesting autobiographers. All his books bear the unmistakable stamp of his stylish, witty, rather formal English prose and abound with original and provocative remarks, keenly observed and gracefully phrased, memorable gleanings from whatever the subject at hand brought to his extraordinary mind.

In his own day, Santayana had many admirers and readers, although the assurance and insolence with which he sought his own way irritated his more earnest philosophical fellows. His contempt for their science, their systems, their colleges and schools, their politics, their logic, and their pretensions caused him to be at best uneasily regarded by the run of his colleagues, and he took care to ensure that no one ever mistook him for one of them. Having decided that difference was his natural lot, Santayana turned it to his advantage. He claimed to consider every topic, including the topics of philosophy, from outside the prevailing conventions. At the very moment when philosophy was questioning its own sources of power and generalization (everywhere asking, What do we mean when we say this?), Santayana seized with maddening confidence the very ground his fellows were scrupulously deserting. He reclaimed philosophy as a pleasure, at a time when philosophy had ceased to be something someone might want to pursue in the regular course of a civilized life, on a sunny day, in a beautiful place, in good company, with a light heart, confident of being the better for the pleasure of it. It is interesting to note that this very appetite has revived in Americans; that is what the New Age aims for, but characteristically, with the expectation of practical use attached to it, another reason to reread George Santayana.

Santayana preferred to live on his own, associating with friends, attractive men, talented, cultivated, curious, wealthy people, predominantly expatriate Americans, migrating rather than nesting. His understanding of the philosophical life borrowed from the peripatetic and the gentlemanly. He divided his time, as he did his mild allegiances, between the Latin and northern countries. He lived most happily in Spain and Italy but was most absorbed by America and England, absorbed and attracted, rebuffed and rebuffing. His old and New English sojourns and acculturation gave him an unnatural perspective on his *patria*. In turn, the perspective his *patria* gave him on the lands of his adoption was critically important. He really did see things about America, and perhaps also about England, in a way that few others have done. He came to America and England, to modern life, from a medieval setting in Avila, where his best chance of getting on would have been to join a Spanish establishment, against the received Enlightenment wisdom of his father. He saw through his father's dogmatic liberalism, while also being prevented by his emigration and his nature from taking up the conventional Spanish life in automatic oedipal reaction. He was thrown from his mother's narrow perch into the commercial and cultural capital of a new imperium, without being able to make its cause his own: America, after all, won its imperial spurs from Spain while Santayana was in early middle age. To be on the fringe, even of the center, was his fate.

Santayana spent his formative intellectual years as a foreign student in a New England that was branching out and dying out. The old New England fierceness that had made so much of American commerce and culture was being supplanted by the large energies, capitalist rather than commercial, democratic rather than genteel, that the world has come to know so well. Santayana was so placed, almost uniquely, as to regret ancient traditions without sentimentalizing them, to criticize modern conditions without refusing to live in them. His loyalties were diluted as well as divided, and he was alienated in one way or another from them all. He came early to a powerfully defensive insight into whatever might lay claim to him. In his clear-eyed way he refused to substitute one allegiance for another, refused to fantasize, as Henry Adams or Walter Pater did, the substitution for the present of some past. He was as detached from what he cherished as from what he criticized. Neither the present nor the past struck Santayana as susceptible of improvement.

In accounting for his particular perspective, Santayana never addressed his homosexuality. His autobiography is not coy about his attraction to men. His biographer, John McCormick, concludes that he was homosexual but for sound social and personal reasons unwilling to risk what was in his day at best a precarious preference. Male friendships formed the core of Santayana's affectional life. He stopped writing poetry because of what he dared not reveal. His novel *The Last Puritan* comes alive in the relationship between Oliver Aldon and his father's ship captain, Lord Jim. Their relationship moves through the range of feeling from sexual captivation through the disappointments of an unacknowledged and unconsummated love affair to an ambivalent, sentimental friendship of the kind Santayana himself had with the second Earl Russell, the great passion of his adult life. The narrowing of emotional response, the insistent detachment in his personal relations, and the persistent animus Santayana felt toward the worlds he inhabited and the people he met suggest that he was not so calm in his renunication of his own sexual nature after all.

The glass closet in which Santayana lived contributed decisively to his understanding of the genteel tradition, and it remains remarkable how many stones he dared to throw. His genteel tradition essays comprise a brilliant account of the way in which America's gendered spheres determined its cultural life. The genteel tradition was "feminine," the alternative world of commerce and activity was "masculine." American homosexuals were to be found in both worlds. The genteel hosted the cultivated, high-minded world, familiar to the readers of Henry James, in which a certain kind of man might thrive in ambiguous but important association with women.

Gay men were also central to the world of men, albeit on less open terms. This was, after all, Whitman and Horatio Alger's terrain. Santayana disdained the genteel but understood how little there was for him in the alternative. The genteel tradition essays play out his predicament. His appreciation of endeavor, material energy, and sports is limited by his own understanding of their intellectual and spiritual limitations. It is a game of desire finally not worth the tumble. The genteel tradition is preoccupied with co-opting the material in the name of beauty and truth. Its sacrifice of the contemplative for the activism of control vitiated it into a caricature of everything it claimed to revere, rendering it blind to what he believed was attractive and important about American activity.

Undergirding Santayana's Americanist writings was a simultaneous attraction to and revulsion from American civilization itself. His detachment allowed him to transcend what he had to renounce, to mend his broken heart by means of dispassionate, superior judgment. Observing well was his best revenge. We have become so accustomed to talking about outsider perspectives that we have perhaps lost a firm sense of what outside and inside really mean in terms of American civilization. For us, outsider has become a category of prospective insider, a figment of injustice. Santayana's outsider status was a path of resistance to inclusion, not a perspective that a more democratic and just society would mediate. Whatever its sources, it did not amount to terms on which he might come home.

Santayana's independence of America was astonishing, arrogant, and attractive. Reading him, one feels that it is possible to fashion from the philosophical traditions of the West an individual philosophical apprehension of life itself. In comparison, the tradition of Tocqueville's perspective seems antique and even obtuse. For unlike the Frenchman, Santayana had a stake in and a taste for American civilization. He was brilliantly perceptive exactly where Tocqueville failed, in the cultural specifics of American life. His observations grounded his abstractions, while in Tocqueville the theory magnetized the observations. What Santayana liked about America were the athletes and the college life, the life of young men, before business and family life and age compromised what he loved in them. He was in the odd position of championing about the United States the very modern and rude energies that were not really congenial to him, because he saw them as native and the genteel as alien to America. He dismissed the genteel because it took all the stuffing from the philosophic, spiritual and emotional, that he valued. But the United States of his day could not satisfy his own tastes.

Influential though they have been, these remarkable essays have been routinely misapprehended. Van Wyck Brooks appropriated Santayana's genteel tradition in *America's Coming of Age*. He, like most Americanists, recast Santayana's analysis as cultural activism, as if it were an agenda for reform. There is little reason to think that Santayana believed the situation he analyzed was susceptible to reform. Indeed, it is possible to read the critics who thought they were learning from Santayana as inevitably extending the problem he observed. Santayana's understanding of the American cultural situation is treacherous to include in an American Studies framework because the useful insights he provided are subversive. The genteel tradition is not one that can be relegated to a period. Santayana's fundamental rejection of the Jeffersonian synthesis of use and beauty informs his analysis of the genteel tradition.

For Santayana the useful is exactly not what the highest pleasures of the human soul invite. They are superior to and unrelated to the useful. Even Tocqueville was not so radical in his rejection of the useful because, unlike Santayana, the Frenchman was much persuaded by the Enlightenment. For Santayana, even the Renaissance was not safe. Knowledge is not power, but the only way to transcend the temptation and delusion of power. The alternative to American activity that it proposes is not a reformed activity, but contemplative inaction. The things that people hoped to achieve through the genteel tradition were not worthy objectives in Santayana's view. The poor were not particularly improved by economic equality; the majority of people were better suited to doing than being. The risk of democracy to contemplation was graver in Santayana's view than the potential benefits to humankind of what even Tocqueville recognized as democracy's virtues. Santayana did not insist on such views, but they secured his understanding of the genteel tradition. He did not suggest, as Americanists did, that once understood, the genteel tradition might be supplanted. Of the great Americanists only Perry Miller understood Santayana's stubbornness about use. Miller was unusual too in his lack of enthusiasm for Tocqueville because Tocqueville did not see the history of American religion and literature as tragic declensions. Social history and issues of race, gender, and class are proper alternatives to Miller's study. They use the tools that replaced the piety that interested him.

Miller saw American moral tragedy resulting in the triumph of American moralism and its frantic, frustrated attempts to control the popular energies as if moralism could be equated with the sterner mysteries of Puritan piety. This much he learned from Santayana. It is exactly what Brooks and the Americanist critics could not learn since their own point was a cultural activism that poured Marxist, liberal, feminist, or humanist wine into vintage moralist bottles. The essence of Santayana's understanding of American civilization remains its unapologetic quietism.

It is hard to think of an American or an Americanist view that can comprehend Santayana's. It is possible that the postmodern applies. It would take a postmodern sensibility to combine the skyscraper and the federal mansion into a shared sensibility. But the postmodern takes the moment seriously and does not, as Santayana claimed he did, see life from the point of view of the grave. Santayana deplored American attempts to put things to use and the postmodern has garnered whimsy for utility. Santayana did not believe in the American university system because it hoped to reconcile the irreconcilable. The traditionally genteel is ever ready to compromise in order to co-opt. The staying power of Santayana's analysis results from its irreducible challenge to *any* American cultural tradition that would co-opt it.

The question remains, however, of how to read Santayana, how, that is, to escape the trap he set for anybody who would try to make use of his insight. One must also ponder the effect of an individuality founded on a detachment so narrowing of human choice and community. It is worth noting that Santayana got his full measure of experience. He understood Whitman as well as Dante. Santayana thought of himself as detached in some Greek philosophical sense from the ordinary claims of life, thus uniquely able to comment upon them, unbounded by the horizons that ordinary attachments create. We may be persuaded that he was detached. But we may note with what unceasing animus his detachment proceeded and remark that the energy of his detachment is every bit as interesting as the calm he claimed for it.

I have a suggestion about how to read Santayana, especially these essays. I think people should read the essays the way we are no longer encouraged to read serious things, with the same gusto, relaxation, and willfulness with which one reads for pleasure. Don't take notes, for goodness sake, lose those yellow markers. The essays make grateful reading. Their arguments are spun out with humor and bewitching mastery. "Young Sammy's Wild Oats" is a happy reminder that no writer or reader is always at his best. Resist conclusions. Try not be become attached to whatever the essays suggest to you at first. Read Santayana as if you were the lay American to whom he condescended, the genteel American he mocked, but don't forget to read it as if you were he and indulge your own possibility of philosophic calm. Indulge in reflection without the temptation or brake of punditry.

It is illuminating to map one's own responses. For years it was "The Genteel Tradition in American Philosophy" that centered my interest in these essays. Much to my surprise, it is now "The Genteel Tradition at Bay" that proccupies me. There is no answer here, no line of explication. Lapidary, the essays are faceted, and their glints should not be taken for enlightenment. The subtlety of Santayana's views or their inconsistency, if you think of it that way, inheres in their constant relation to an inconstant but consistent culture. Despite their decorous surfaces, the essays are not beholden to a view of action and in that way resemble the Americanist writing of D. H. Lawrence and William Carlos Williams, similarly freed from bogus responsibility. The unique quality of Santayana's essays lies in their sly, seductive invitation to consider one's own civilization as if it didn't "construct" one, as we say now. Imagine that you might be that individual hardly anyone seems to credit any more, a human being whose essence is having a soul and a nature and a will, the exercise of which is the highest pleasure, uncorrupted by conscience and community.

Rereading these essays, I realized again how my own habitual "use" of them is at odds with my experience of them. When I forget my training in momentary surrender to the delights of Santayana's essays, I free myself to see things from a truly other point of view. The genteel tradition survives palpably in my own Jeffersonian academic liberal earnestness. But these essays give me moments when I see my own views for what they are. As a gay man, whose sense of himself is rooted in the contemporary understanding of sexual orientation and identity, I can see how partial that view is, essential to my politics but perhaps insufficient for my humanity. It is important for me to see why I really do believe in liberal democracy, why the Enlightenment persuades me, why the university continues to move me. Reading these essays, I must acknowledge how provincial and patriotic I am and shall remain. Unlike most cultural criticism, these essays reward the reader with a sharp apprehension of the limitations of the American subject and subject position. I emphasize the individual experience of reading Santayana on the genteel tradition for two reasons. First, it is the individual, not the culture, whose modern predicament interested him. Second, it is the individual, not the culture, we have gotten out of the habit of imagining.

Contents

Preface

George Santayana's career as a writer was considerably more diverse than is usually recognized. He is known and remembered first of all as a philosopher, yet he began his career as a poet. Before he abandoned poetry, he had also written a handful of plays in verse. He wrote a distinguished novel, *The Last Puritan*, which has continued to attract readers for over thirty years; his autobiography *Persons and Places* has been called a classic of the genre and compared with those of Franklin and Henry Adams; and throughout his career he was an acknowledged master of the essay. The present collection, however, is not designed to reflect this dazzling diversity, but rather the editor has undertaken to mine, from the vast lode of Santayana's writings, a single vein. Assembled here are the products of one of Santayana's most memorable preoccupations—the genteel tradition in America.

Most of the pieces were written over a span of ten years
—roughly speaking, the decade 1910-1920. This is an interesting and indicative fact, not merely for the light it
sheds on this period of Santayana's own life and career,
but also for the significance it holds for our understanding of the same period in the life of American culture.
For these essays form no less than a vital part of the
lively ferment over cultural self-appraisal that dominated
the American intellectual scene during those and succeeding years. As such, they may be more clearly viewed,
when brought together as they are here, as constituting
yet another aspect of Santayana's substantial American
legacy.

While there are passages to be found throughout his published works that bear on this theme, only pieces complete in themselves have been included. The result which
is offered in these pages consists of eight essays and a
poem—or perhaps more properly, nine essays, one of
which is in verse. All of these pieces, with the exception
of "The Moral Background," were originally published
in periodicals. Five of them were later revised and published in hard cover by the author. The other three were
never collected by the author and were allowed to repose
in the periodicals as "fugitives." All of the pieces are re-
produced from their original place of publication and in
their original form. Typographical errors have been silently corrected.

The editor's indebtedness for assistance on this project is
greater than can be properly acknowledged here, but the
largest debts are these: to Mr. Daniel Cory, Charles
Scribner's Sons, J. M. Dent and Sons, Ltd., and Constable

and Co., Ltd., for permission to reprint Santayana's writings; to Knox College and its generous faculty research program for making available funds and facilities; to Dean Hermann R. Muelder, the administrator of that program for his continuing support and encouragement; to Professor Robert E. Spiller of the University of Pennsylvania for the suggestion which led to the present collection and for helpful advice and assistance along the way; to Professor James Ballowe of Bradley University for his special knowledge; to Knox College Librarian Warren Mac Morris and his staff for their constant assistance; and finally the editor is deeply indebted to his wife Sharon whose abundant good works have been exceeded in value only by her abounding faith.

Galesburg, Illinois   Douglas L. Wilson
March 1967

The Genteel Tradition

Nine Essays by George Santayana

Introductory

I

At what now appears to have been precisely the right moment, George Santayana introduced into the American cultural dialogue a phrase and an idea that were destined to make a difference. They were destined to affect the tone as well as the substance of what was becoming, in the early years of this century, an increasingly urgent dialogue and to help focus the attention of a disaffected generation on the nature and character of that with which they were most deeply at odds in the culture they had inherited—the genteel tradition. Whether one should emphasize the peculiar appropriateness of the moment or the compelling aptness of the phrase and idea in accounting for their subsequent impact and influence is not altogether clear. However it may be, both are crucial, and the phrase has become so completely ingrained in the twentieth-century American conception of the immediate past that Lionel Trilling has asserted flatly: "what the historian of American culture would do without Santayana's term 'the genteel tradition' is impossible to imagine."[1]

Santayana came at his subject from an angle peculiarly his own, and how he came to make such an utterance at the moment that he did amounts to a cultural accident. He never accepted America or its culture as his own; he was truly an alien right from the time that his Spanish father brought him to the United States at the age of eight to remain and be reared by his Spanish mother, whose first husband had been a Boston merchant. Neither Boston, where he was raised, nor Harvard, where he was educated and taught for over twenty years, was congenial to his Spanish temperament and he escaped their chafing effects by traveling in Europe whenever he could. Privately, Santayana was capable of scoring the institutions of American culture in bitter terms. In 1900, he wrote to William James, his former teacher and then colleague in the Philosophy department at Harvard: "You tax me several times with impertinence and superior airs. I wonder if you realize the years of suppressed irritation which I have past [sic] in the midst of an unintelligible sanctimonious and often disingenous Protestantism, which is thoroughly alien and repulsive to me . . ."[2] But publicly he either was too diffident or too polite to ruffle the feathers of Boston and Harvard with such plain speaking. It was, for example, a genuine relief to him to deliver a series of lectures in English at the Sorbonne in 1905, for he

---

[1] " 'That Smile of Parmenides Made Me Think,' " A Gathering of Fugitives (Boston: Beacon Press, 1956), p. 157.
[2] The Letters of George Santayana, ed. Daniel Cory (New York: Charles Scribner's Sons, 1955), p. 62.

wrote to James: "The freedom of speaking in a foreign language among foreigners—I mean the intellectual room—is exhilerating. You can say what is *really true*. You needn't remember that you are in Cambridge, or are addressing the youth entrusted to your personal charge. I have never felt so grown up as I do at the Sorbonne; after our atmosphere, this is liberty."[3]

But Santayana's moment for speaking out in public eventually came. In 1911, at the University of California at Berkeley, where he had accepted a teaching position in the summer session, he was duly invited to address the Philosophical Union. As he indicated in a letter to a friend, he had accepted the California appointment as "probably the last chance I should have"[4] to see California and the Pacific; his mind seems already to have been made up not to return from his forthcoming sabbatical leave abroad. Separated from New England by the breadth of an entire continent and about to take permanent leave of America, Santayana was thus presented with the right time and place for saying, as he told his audience, "something I have long wanted to say which this occasion seems particularly favorable for saying."[5] What he said was apparently quite unexpected even among those who knew him intimately, for writing a

[3] *Letters*, p. 80.
[4] *Letters*, p. 105.
[5] "The Genteel Tradition in American Philosophy," *University of California Chronicle*, XII:4 (October 1911), 357. Recently, this address has been described as "fully as important a document in the study of American culture as Emerson's 'The American Scholar' or Frederick Jackson Turner's 'The Significance of the Frontier in American History.'" Joe Lee Davis, "Santayana as a Critic of Transcendentalism," *Transcendentalism and its Legacy*, ed. Myron Simon and Thornton H. Parsons (Ann Arbor: University of Michigan Press, 1966), p. 160.

few months later to his sister, to whom he had probably
sent a copy or account of the address, he asked:

Where did you get the impression that anything in California
could have affected my opinions or sentiments? When there . . .
I felt almost out of America, so much so that I once said inad-
vertently to someone in San Francisco that I soon had to go back
to America. That is why, from [there], I felt like expressing myself: because when I am here [Cambridge] in the midst of a
dull round, a sort of instinct of courtesy makes me take it for
granted, and I become unconscious of how much I hate it all:
otherwise I couldn't have stood it for *forty years!*[6]

The address he delivered on August 25, the most incisive
piece he was to write on the subject, was "The Genteel
Tradition in American Philosophy."

Santayana's address, whose title phrase would shortly become famous, was thus an accident in space and time as
well as personal circumstances; had he not found himself in
California with an invitation to speak at that propitious moment, he would almost certainly have left the country
having said nothing. "But accidents," as Santayana was to
write in another connection, "are accidents only to ignorance; in reality all physical events flow out of one another
by a continuous intertwined derivation . . ."[7] In 1911, as
Santayana was putting down his analysis of the malady of
American intellectual life, a whole generation was awaken-
ing to the deficiencies of its literary and intellectual heritage
—a generation that was to mount a critical onslaught that
would precipitate a cultural revolution. It was the point in
time that Van Wyck Brooks was a few years later to desig-

[6] *Letters,* p. 110.
[7] *Persons and Places: The Background of My Life* (New York:
Charles Scribner's Sons, 1944), p. 2.

nate hopefully as "America's coming-of-age." A more recent analysis has seen it as the point that marked the beginning of "the end of American innocence."[8] The moment for Santayana's attractive phrase—and the theory that went with it—was ripe.

In spite of the "philosophy" in its title, Santayana's address was as much if not more concerned with the American tradition in literature. He had begun his career as a poet and had turned to philosophy—what he called his "alternative tradition"—only when circumstances, personal and cultural, conspired to deprive him of his muse, so that he was keenly sensitive to the shortcomings of the American literary milieu. He had been part of the Harvard school of poets in the nineties who had tried—and failed—to rejuvenate American poetry by a radical reversion to classical models and methods. Not able to recognize that this movement was actually the last gasp of an exhausted Romantic mode, Santayana persisted in thinking that its failure was due to the cultural environment, what he referred to as "a lack of air to breathe."[9] This was a crucial factor in focusing his attention on the nation's intellectual underpinnings in such a way that he came to regard gentility as the prime enemy of a vigorous and imaginative cultural life and to think that American thought and letters were plagued by a genteel tradition.

Santayana's strictures were welcomed by the younger, resurgent generation, once they became known, not only because they expressed something important and useful, but

[8] Henry F. May, *The End of American Innocence: A Study of the First Years of Our Own Time 1912-1917* (New York: Alfred A. Knopf, 1957). This far-ranging work cannot be recommended too highly to anyone interested in the period.
[9] *Letters*, p. 306.

because they put the "custodians of culture"[10] on the defensive. Writing in the *Atlantic Monthly* a few years after Santayana's address appeared in book form, Randolph Bourne, the most brilliant spokesman of the younger generation, took note of "the guarded defenses and discreet apologies for the older generation which keep filtering through the essays of the *Atlantic*."

It is always an encouraging sign [Bourne wrote] when people are rendered self-conscious and are forced to examine the basis of their ideals. The demand that they explain them to skeptics always makes for clarity. When the older generation is put on the defensive, it must first discover what convictions it has, and then sharpen them to their finest point in order to present them convincingly. There are always too many unquestioned things in the world, and for a person or class to have to scurry about to find reasons for its prejudices is about as healthy an exercise as one could wish for either of them . . . This always indicates that something has begun to slide, that the world is no longer so secure as it was, that obvious truths are no longer obvious, that the world has begun to bristle with question marks.[11]

Certainly one of the most valuable effects that Santayana's theory of the genteel tradition was to have was to make the established world less secure and the received views less obvious.

Toward the social smugness, the intellectual complacency, and the thorough-going gentility of this older generation, Bourne and the whole host of writers typified by him

---

[10] See May, pp. 30-51.
[11] "This Older Generation," *The History of a Literary Radical and Other Essays*, ed. Van Wyck Brooks (New York: B. W. Huebsch, 1920), pp. 107, 108-09.

adopted an attitude of radical disaffection that was to have an important residual effect upon succeeding generations of young artists. So pervasive and important was this development that a recent commentator has seen it as the source in American literary history of the self-conscious posture that we are accustomed to call "alienation." In describing this phenomenon in the introduction to his book, *After Alienation*, Marcus Klein writes:

"Alienation" I take to begin in that deliberate strategy of discontent, almost a program, which was enunciated just before World War I by Van Wyck Brooks and Randolph Bourne, which informed if it did not entirely account for famous episodes in our modern literature like the *Risorgimento*, and the Lost Generation, the Younger Generation, and Disillusion, which then was inherited and put to the uses of revolution by the proletarian 1930's, which finally was the dominant mode of our literature until just yesterday, some time after World War II. It is the theory, not necessarily enunciated, of something more than a generation of our *avant-gardes*.[12]

Mr. Klein's suggestion, that the attitude adopted by these writers continued to affect succeeding literary generations, however adequate or inadequate its formulation, serves to underline the importance of the movement for which Santayana's critique of the genteel tradition was welcome ammunition.

The groundwork for this movement, and much of the inspiration for it, came, of course, not from men like Santayana, who refused to believe in progress or democracy, but from the "liberal ideology" emanating from the work of

[12] *After Alienation* (Cleveland and New York: Meridian Books, 1965), p. 17.

men like John Dewey, Thorstein Veblen, and Charles Beard.[13] These writers, all professors, symbolized the arrival of a new spirit in the academy as well as the country at large. It was in this spirit and in this period that another professor, Vernon Parrington, began a monumental effort of cultural reappraisal which would eventually emerge more than a decade later as *Main Currents in American Thought*. A veritable avalanche of New Poetry was let loose, filling countless little magazines that had to be founded to accommodate it, just as the *New Republic*, the *Masses*, the *Seven Arts* and the new *Dial* had to be established to accommodate the critical prose. Recalling this period only a few years later in a memoir of Bourne, Van Wyck Brooks testified, "It was a tremendous moment. Never had we realized so keenly the spiritual inadequacy of American life: the great war of the cultures left us literally gasping in the vacuum of our own provincialism, colonialism, naiveté, and romantic self-complacency."[14] The time could not have been more ripe for a vivid and telling characterization of the genteel tradition.

II

Santayana's criticism of America has sometimes been discounted and even discredited by cultural historians as coming from a biased and unsympathetic quarter. Noting

[13] See Morton White, *Social Thought in America: The Revolt Against Formalism* (Boston: Beacon Press, 1957).
[14] "Introduction," *History of a Literary Radical*, p. xix. Reprinting this essay later in *Emerson and Others* (New York: E. P. Dutton and Co., 1927), Brooks silently toned down "tremendous" to "interesting." For an account of the period from the point of view of literary history, see Robert E. Spiller et al, *Literary History of the United States*, 3 vols. (New York: The Macmillan Company, 1948), particularly chapters 67 and 68, "Creating an Audience" and "The Battle of the Books."

that he is no champion of democracy, they like to make him out, as Lionel Trilling has neatly put it, as "the Gilbert Osmond of their *Portrait of a Lady,* the Lady being America . . ." But while he was aristocratic in his outlook and openly critical of democracy, those who would cast Santayana in such a role, as Trilling points out, "are much mistaken . . . America, it is true, seemed to have affected him adversely in almost a physical way, making him anxious and irritable. But it was to a particular aspect of American life that he directed his antagonism, the aspect of its high culture."[15] Trilling's point is well taken and particularly apt, for it is important to bear in mind above all else that Santayana formulated his theory of the genteel tradition preeminently as an attempt to diagnose the shortcomings of American intellectual life and its feeble creation, American high culture.

Santayana's theory of the genteel tradition begins in an attempt to account for a certain doubleness in the American mind, "a curious alternation and irrelevance," he once called it, "as between weekdays and Sabbaths, between American ways and American opinions."[16] Other important elements figure into his analysis, as the reader of these essays will discover, but the idea of doubleness, of a split in the national mind, of a kind of separation of mental powers, is central to his whole conception of the American intellect and its works.

Santayana was well aware that he was not the first to point out this doubleness, nor is it as a *discovery* that his formu-

---

[15] Trilling, pp. 156-57.
[16] "The Moral Background," *Character and Opinion in the United States* (New York: Charles Scribner's Sons, 1920), p. 7.

lation has become influential and important. It is perhaps
a small irony that the man who was in many ways the personification and voice of the genteel tradition, Theodore
Roosevelt, had delivered a series of lectures, also in Berkeley and also in 1911, only a few months before Santayana's
address, in which he remarked: "I chose as the opening
lecture this address on realizable ideals, because the longer
I have lived the more strongly I have felt the harm done
by the practice among so many men of keeping their consciences in separate compartments; sometimes a Sunday
conscience and a week-day conscience: sometimes a conscience as to what they do and like other people to do;
sometimes a conscience for their private affairs and a totally
different conscience for their business relations."[17] Had
Santayana had no more to say than this, his address, like
the ex-president's, would have been quickly forgotten, and
the "revolt against gentility," as Malcolm Cowley was to
call it, would have had to proceed without the benefit of
his incisive mind. Santayana's contribution was far more
considerable than merely pointing out what many other
people had already observed. His contribution, appropriate
to his position and stature, was to give a philosophical account of the origin, development, and character of a serious
defect in American cultural and intellectual experience.

Near the beginning of the Berkeley address, Santayana
summarizes the theory of the genteel tradition as succinctly
as he was ever to do:

America is not simply, as I said a moment ago, a young country
with an old mentality: it is a country with two mentalities, one

[17] *Realizable Ideals* (The Earl Lectures), *The Works of Theodore
Roosevelt*, National Edition, 20 vols. (New York: Charles Scribner's
Sons, 1926), XIII, 616. These lectures are referred to in May, p. 17.

a survival of the beliefs and standards of the fathers, the other an expression of the instincts, practice, and discoveries of the younger generations. In all the higher things of the mind—in religion, in literature, in the moral emotions—it is the hereditary spirit that still prevails, so much so that Mr. Bernard Shaw finds that America is a hundred years behind the times. The truth is that that one-half of the American mind, that not occupied intensely in practical affairs, has remained, I will not say high-and-dry, but slightly becalmed; it has floated gently in the back-water, while, alongside, in invention and industry and social organization the other half of the mind was leaping down a sort of Niagara Rapids. This division may be found symbolized in American architecture: a neat reproduction of the colonial mansion—with some modern comforts introduced surreptitiously —stands beside the sky-scraper. The American Will inhabits the sky-scraper; the American Intellect inhabits the colonial mansion. The one is the sphere of the American man; the other, at least predominantly, of the American woman. The one is all aggressive enterprise; the other is all genteel tradition.[18]

It might be said that this is, to some extent, an enlargement of Emerson's remark that "our people have their intellectual culture from one country and their duties from another."[19] But Santayana's distinction is much finer and it carries the idea a good deal further, insisting as it does on the magnitude of the disparities and dramatizing their deep-seated presence in the life around us. Moreover, Santayana's distinction emphasizes that the two mentalities constitute a single mind and suggests the interrelationship between the weaknesses of the American mind and its strengths. Once this point has been grasped, its consequences in terms of dangers and shortcomings in American

[18] "Genteel Tradition in American Philosophy," *University of California Chronicle,* pp. 358-59.
[19] Cited in Van Wyck Brooks, "America's Coming-of-Age," *Three Essays on America* (New York: E. P. Dutton and Co., 1934), p. 22.

life can be readily discerned. Malcolm Cowley, following
Van Wyck Brooks, has demonstrated how this divided
mentality might manifest itself in the behavior of a single
man. The example is Andrew Carnegie, "who made a fortune by manufacturing armor plate and then spent it in
promoting peace by impractical methods and in building
libraries where the men in his rolling mills, who worked
twelve hours a day and seven days a week, would never
have time to read the master-works. Culture was something
reserved and refined for the Sunday people: women, min-
isters, university professors and the readers of genteel
magazines."[20]

A close look at Santayana's summary of the dualities in the
American mind reveals that the poet-philosopher's imagery
not only establishes the tone but quietly passes judgments:
a "survival" rather than an "expression," a "back-water"
alongside a "Niagara," a nostalgic "reproduction" over
against a towering modern structure, and finally the feminine and passive as opposed to the masculine and aggressive. The characteristic vividness of Santayana's images and
the deftness with which they delineate the antinomies of
American life are of course important factors in the attrac-
tiveness and success of his thesis. Santayana's metaphors,
like those of any good poet, are considerably more than so
much decorative bric-a-brac; they radiate implications,
they breed meanings. But in addition to this, Santayana's
imagery relentlessly seeks out the most vulnerable aspects
of his subject, quickening in the responsive reader his

[20] "The Revolt Against Gentility," *After the Genteel Tradition* (Car-
bondale: Southern Illinois University Press, 1964), p. ii. For this
reissue of a book originally published in 1937, Cowley revised this
essay which appears as a foreword to the book.

awareness of the sources of his own discontent and confirming and justifying his sense of alienation from the proprietors of the genteel establishment. A prosaic account of equal validity would have been incapable of attracting the interest or exerting the influence that Santayana's actually did. Passing on from the original address, let us consider some illustrations of Santayana's strategic imagery in essays that were to appear subsequently.

The identification of the genteel tradition with a predominantly feminine sensibility—one that is passive, decorous, delicate, apart from the on-going business of society—is comic yet serious and pervasive. Consider his description, for British audiences, of American public schooling: "The child passes very young into a free school, established and managed by the municipal authorities; the teachers, even for the older boys, are chiefly unmarried women, sensitive, faithful, and feeble; their influence helps to establish that separation which is so characteristic of America between things intellectual, which remain wrapped in a feminine veil and, as it were, under glass, and the rough passions of life."[21] Also, the genteel tradition at its most entrenched is usually represented, in keeping with his theory of the old and young America, as a superannuated mentality, or as outright senility. The opening of *Character and Opinion in the United States* (1920) is an example: "About the middle of the nineteenth century, in the quiet sunshine of provincial prosperity, New England had an Indian summer of the mind; and an agreeable reflective literature showed how brilliant that russet and yellow season could be. There were poets, historians, orators, preachers, most of whom

[21] "The Academic Environment," *Character and Opinion*, p. 44.

had studied foreign literatures and had travelled; they demurely kept up with the times; they were universal humanists. But it was all a harvest of leaves; these worthies had
an expurgated and barren conception of life; theirs was
the purity of sweet old age."[22]

Accordingly, Santayana's description-indictment is at its
most devastating when these two images, the feminine and
the superannuated, are fused and the genteel tradition is
personified as a kind of senile femininity. Thus, his description of "genteel American poetry": "It was simple,
sweet, humane, Protestant literature, grandmotherly in that
sedate spectacled wonder with which it gazed at this terrible world and said how beautiful and how interesting it
all was."[23] In a single blow, the mindless cheer, the intellectual myopia, and the spiritual complacency of an entire
tradition in American poetry is rendered ridiculous. Part
of the genius of Santayana's method and the success of his
grandmotherly personification, it should be noted, lies not
in its severity but in its guileless comic nature. Though he
may have had private cause for it, he exhibits publicly no
bitterness. His words are calculated to provoke humor,
though not humor alone.

The value of Santayana's theory of the genteel tradition can
probably be counted as much in inspiration as in insight.
The phrase served not only to focus attention on the most
vulnerable chink in the Establishment's armor, but it also
served the "literary radicals" as a rallying cry in their insurgent war on intellectual poverty. Gentility, as a conse-

[22] "The Moral Background," *Character and Opinion*, p. 1.
[23] "Genteel American Poetry," *New Republic*, III:30 (May 29, 1915),
94.

quence, continued to draw sniper fire long after it had been permanently disabled. Meanwhile, Santayana's personification—the bespectacled grandmother—continued to reappear in a multitude of incarnations. She is featured, for example, by one of Santayana's earliest admirers, Wallace Stevens, in the title-role of his poem, "A High-toned Old Christian Woman." She is also enshrined in an early poem of E. E. Cummings, whose father, like Santayana, was a Harvard professor.

> The Cambridge ladies who live in furnished souls
> are unbeautiful and have comfortable minds
> (also, with the church's protestant blessings
> daughters, unscented shapeless spirited)
> they believe in Christ and Longfellow, both dead,
> are invariably interested in so many things—
> at the present writing one still finds
> delighted fingers knitting for the is it Poles?
> perhaps. While permanent faces coyly bandy
> scandal of Mrs. N and Professor D[24]

"Furnished souls" and "comfortable minds" are precisely what the genteel tradition is all about: the unexamined life, the empty allegiance to whatever custom prescribes, the smug complacency (the "permanent faces" of the poem), the meaningless activity that buzzes, like Emily Dickinson's fly, in the presence of the death of the mind.

[24] Copyright, 1923, 1951, by E. E. Cummings. Reprinted from "the Cambridge ladies who live in furnished souls" in *Poems 1923-1954* by E. E. Cummings by permission of Harcourt, Brace and World, Inc.

III

When Santayana left America in January of 1912, he was on an extended leave from his teaching duties at Harvard, part of an arrangement with President Lowell whereby he was obligated, after a year's absence, to teach only the first term of each session. He resigned when his mother's death, less than a month after he sailed, left him free of family attachments in America, and he never returned. By 1913, when "The Genteel Tradition in American Philosophy" became available to the general public in book form, Santayana was permanently settled abroad. The outbreak of war a year later may have obscured somewhat his observations of the kind of impression his genteel tradition thesis was making, though he was much in demand, in both the British and American press, as a commentator on the American scene. He appears to have been aware, to some degree at least, of the currency and force that his phrase was acquiring, as evidenced by his use of *genteel* and *genteel tradition* in subsequent essays. In "Genteel American Poetry," published in 1915, he was still expounding what he meant by a tradition of gentility, using nineteenth-century American poetry as his example. But by 1918, he could say in an address to the British Academy, "Philosophical opinion in America is of course rooted in the genteel tradition,"[25] a remark which clearly takes for granted that the audience may be expected to know what *the* genteel tradition is. A review written for the *Dial* in 1922, "Notes on Civilization in the United States," reveals that Santayana is aware of the powerful potential that his phrase has acquired as an epithet of opprobrium, as he

---

[25] "Philosophical Opinion in America," *British Academy: Proceedings,* VIII (1917-1918), 300.

speaks of witholding the charge of gentility lest it enrage the authors of the book too much. Finally, in "The Genteel Tradition at Bay" (1931), we find him yielding to what had become by then a common temptation to use the phrase as nothing more than a stick with which to beat one's adversaries—in this case, the New Humanists.

Some varied examples of the use that was made by others of Santayana's genteel tradition may serve to suggest the range of its utility and appeal. The literary and cultural historian, Vernon Parrington, who had been at work on his ambitious treatise, *Main Currents of American Thought*, since approximately the time Santayana coined the term and whose discovery of it was apparently early (he cites the Berkeley publication), saw in the genteel tradition the explanation behind the enfeebled culture of the seventies. He wrote: "The inevitable fruit of such thin soil was the genteel tradition, the excellence of which in the seventies New England maintained in the face of all frontier levelling and romantic liberalism—a timid and uncreative culture that lays its inhibitions on every generation that is content to live in the past . . . Yet to the generation of the seventies the inhibitions of the genteel tradition were all-powerful, and the little Boston group set themselves up as a court of final jurisdiction over American letters. New England parochialism had become a nation-wide nuisance."[26]

Another example of the use to which Santayana's genteel tradition was put, very different yet not far removed in time from Parrington's, is found in the Nobel Prize acceptance speech of Sinclair Lewis in 1930. This is an incident

[26] *The Beginnings of Critical Realism* (New York: Harcourt, Brace and Company, 1930), pp. 52-53.

so indicative that Malcolm Cowley builds a whole essay, the introductory to his *After the Genteel Tradition*, around it. In his speech, Lewis not only labels his literary enemies in the American Academy of Arts and Letters as the representatives of the "genteel tradition," he cites them as an "example of the divorce in America of intellectual life from all authentic standards of importance and reality."[27] This is, of course, precisely the keynote of Santayana's concept of the genteel tradition.

A very much later and very different example of the use of Santayana's genteel tradition, and one that demonstrates the enduring utility of the concept, is Leo Marx's use of the term in a well-known essay on *Huckleberry Finn*. Marx is concerned in his essay with the unsatisfactory conclusion of Mark Twain's great novel, and he finds in a passage from "The Genteel Tradition in American Philosophy" the key to its failure. "The unhappy truth about the ending of *Huckleberry Finn*," he says, "is that the author, having revealed the tawdry nature of the culture of the great valley, yielded to its essential complacency." This way of looking at the novel he goes on, "confirms the brilliant insight of George Santayana, who many years ago spoke of American humorists, of whom he considered Mark Twain an outstanding representative, as having only 'half escaped' the genteel tradition. Santayana meant that men like Clemens were able to 'point to what contradicts it in the facts, but

---

[27] "The American Fear of Literature," *Why Sinclair Lewis Got the Nobel Prize* (New York: Harcourt, Brace and Company, 1931), p. 17. An unpublished doctoral dissertation by Danforth Ross ("The Genteel Tradition: Its Characteristics and its Origins," University of Minnesota, 1954), which cites this source, also includes a useful survey of the occurrences of Santayana's phrase.

not in order to abandon the genteel tradition, for they have nothing solid to put in its place' . . . Clemens had presented the contrast between the two social orders but could not, or would not, accept the tragic fact that the one he had rejected was an image of solid reality and the other an ecstatic dream."[28]

These examples from Parrington, Lewis, and Marx are ones in which the indebtedness to Santayana is either openly acknowledged or otherwise direct enough to be fairly obvious. They all explicitly use his phrase genteel tradition, and many similar examples could be presented. Yet the most important debt to Santayana with respect to his idea of the genteel tradition is one that has gone unacknowledged and virtually unrecognized. This is the indebtedness evident in the early writing of Van Wyck Brooks, particularly in the very influential essay, "America's Coming-of-Age." For while Brooks felt no personal or intellectual attraction for Santayana and his views, the effect of Santayana's Berkeley address on his own thinking and writing is demonstrably distinct and unmistakable.

In the first volume of his autobiography, *Scenes and Portraits*, Brooks characterized Santayana, one of the luminaries of his years at Harvard: "He was repelled by everything that characterized American life, preferring a World 'run by cardinals and engineers' rejecting as 'all a harvest of leaves' the New England Renaissance and its best essayists, historians, romancers and poets. His smiling contempt for the efforts of men to better the world and humanity was

[28] "Mr. Eliot, Mr. Trilling, and *Huckleberry Finn*," *The American Scholar*, XXII:4 (Autumn 1953), 432.

reflected in a host of Harvard minds that were reversing the whole tendency of the great New England epoch, dismissing its faith in progress as 'the babble of dreamers.' "[29] This passage suggests rather vividly the distance between Brooks and Santayana, but it further suggests what innumerable references in Brook's other volumes bear out, that he was quite familiar with what Santayana had written about American life; and the evidence makes it pretty clear that, as a young man, Brooks was able to profit immensely from the ideas of his former teacher, while groping for ways to diagnose and prescribe for the malady of American cultural life.

In the summer of 1911, Brooks was married in California and accepted an instructorship at Stanford University. He had close friends across the bay in Berkeley and he may well have been in the audience when, in August, Santayana delivered his celebrated address before the Philosophical Union. Or, not having been present, he almost certainly would have heard about the address and read it when it was published a few months later in the *University of California Chronicle*. That he was familiar with it and that it profoundly affected the characterization of our intellectual tradition that he was to offer a few years later in "America's Coming-of-Age" (1915), no one who has compared the two essays will want to deny. To review the points of comparison which reflect Brooks's indebtedness to Santayana's essay is to recount a series, not of borrowings and much less of thefts, but of modulations of phrases, metaphors, and ideas. The most telling of these points of comparison

[29] *Scenes and Portraits: Memories of Childhood and Youth* (New York: Dutton, 1954), p. 106.

are found in the initial section, "'Highbrow' and 'Low-brow,'" the best known section of the essay, which was printed separately in the *Forum*. There Santayana's notion of the split in the American mind is appropriated by Brooks, modulated, and presented as the key to an understanding of the crisis in American culture. Using the vernacular "highbrow" and "lowbrow" to designate the two "attitudes of mind" one finds in America, he asks "What side of American life is not touched by this antithesis? What explanation of American life is more central and more illuminating? In everything one finds this frank acceptance of twin values which are not expected to have anything in common: on the one hand, a quite unclouded, quite unhypocritical assumption of transcendent theory ("high ideals"), on the other a simultaneous acceptance of catchpenny realities. Between university ethics and business ethics, between American culture and American humour, between Good Government and Tammany, between academic pedantry and pavement slang, there is no community, no genial middle ground."[30]

This is considerably more substantial than Teddy Roosevelt's commonplaces and somewhat different, in tone and emphasis, from Santayana, but as a description of a state of affairs, it is at one with Santayana's and begins at precisely the same point: a single America with a divided mentality. Brooks then goes on to give an account of the origin of this division, and here again we note the closeness to Santayana's account, including an echo, in the image of

[30] "America's Coming-of-Age," pp. 17-18. May perceptively notes that Brooks's highbrow-lowbrow distinction was "essentially Santayana's" (p. 324). Sherman Paul has pointed out the California juxtaposition of Brooks and Santayana in unpublished material.

"main currents" (later picked up by Parrington), of Santayana's metaphor of the "back-water" and the "Niagara Rapids." But Brooks turns the idea to his own purposes and, in so doing, brings forth the now familiar comparison of Edwards and Franklin:

So it is that from the beginning we find two main currents in the American mind running side by side but rarely mingling—a current of overtones and a current of undertones—and both equally unsocial: on the one hand, the transcendental current, originating in the piety of the Puritans, becoming a philosophy in Jonathan Edwards, passing through Emerson, producing the fastidious refinement and aloofness of the chief American writers, and resulting in the final unreality of most contemporary American culture; and on the other hand the current of catchpenny opportunism, originating in the practical shifts of Puritan life, becoming a philosophy in Franklin, passing through the American humorists, and resulting in the atmosphere of our contemporary business life.[31]

Brooks's tone, it should be noted, unlike Santayana's, which is comparatively detached and disinterested, is that of one very much disturbed by the state of affairs he is describing. Indeed, one of the main purposes of the essay is to suggest a program for improvement, something at best incidental to Santayana's purpose. But what the one owes to the other is clearly discernible, nonetheless, at point after point.

Another telling parallel between Brooks's essay and Santayana's Berkeley address is their treatment of the situation of the genuinely talented writers of the nineteenth century. Santayana had said that such writers—he specifically named Poe, Hawthorne, and Emerson—were in "great straits" be-

[31] "America's Coming-of-Age," p. 19.

cause they could not "retail the genteel tradition," being "too keen, too perceptive, and too independent for that."[32] "They were fastidious," he said, and, because of their situation, their writing had a "starved and abstract quality." Pointing to the same three men, Brooks says that they turned from the rudeness of actuality to a "disembodied world . . . a world fastidiously intellectual . . ." In the same section of his essay, one also finds Brooks speaking of "two publics" in America, "the one largely feminine, the other largely masculine."[33]

Throughout his essay, Brooks can be seen to be using Santayana's ideas or phrases as points of departure, but the point of documenting this indebtedness at such length is not simply that Brooks himself does not acknowledge it, but that what Brooks had to say was to have a tremendous influence on the younger writers, the same men who would precipitate the literary and cultural revolution of the twenties which effectively broke the hold of the genteel tradition on American high culture. The Brooks of this period, Edmund Wilson has written, was "probably, for the writers of these years, the principle source of ideas on the cultural life of the United States. People got from him, not only, as they did also from Mencken, a sense of the second-ratedness of recent American writing and a conviction of the need for something better, but also an historical perspective and an analysis of the causes of what was wrong."[34]

In 1937, Malcolm Cowley edited the book of essays, previously referred to, entitled *After the Genteel Tradition*, in

[32] "Genteel Tradition in American Philosophy," p. 362.
[33] "America's Coming-of-Age," pp. 79, 78-79.
[34] "Van Wyck Brooks's Second Phase," *Classics and Commercials* (New York: Farrar, Straus and Company, 1950), p. 11.

which, in addition to the important introductory essay,
Cowley contributed a "literary calendar" which recorded
the important events in the unseating of the genteel tradition from 1911 to 1930. The entries under 1911 do not include the Berkeley address nor is it mentioned elsewhere
in the volume. But under 1915, Cowley writes, "Van Wyck
Brooks sets the tone of the era in *America's Coming-of-
Age*."[35] There is, of course, nothing surprising in this, nor
has any conscious injustice been done. Cowley and his generation knew that Santayana had coined the term "genteel
tradition," but they had little reason to think that they were
actually and effectively in the debt of someone so unlike
themselves in point of view as he. Nonetheless, Santayana's
essay played a more important role in the movement than
has been realized and deserves a significant place at the
beginning of Cowley's calendar.

Gradually, the term genteel tradition began to wear out its
initial welcome, being constantly invoked in a variety of
contexts and in the service of various causes. By 1942 Alfred Kazin could justifiably complain in *On Native Grounds*
about the mechanical application of "Santayana's well-worn
phrase, the 'Genteel Tradition,' to everything Mencken's
iconoclastic generation disliked in late nineteenth-century
life"; it had become, in his view, a "dead horse."[36] But less
than ten years later, F. O. Matthiessen brilliantly demonstrated that its original, incisive meaning had not been entirely lost in the shuffle of almost forty years. In his book
on Dreiser he warned against the tendency at midcentury

---

[35] *After the Genteel Tradition*, p. 187.
[36] *On Native Grounds* (New York: Reynal and Hitchcock, 1942),
pp. vii, 56.

to develop a "nostalgic longing" for the genteel tradition and reminded his readers that

Santayana coined the phrase "the genteel tradition" to describe what he considered was the most dangerous defect in American thought. Observing our dominant New England culture, Santayana believed that its deep-rooted error was that it separated thought from experience. Among the legacies of a colonial culture is the habit of thinking of creative sources as somehow remote from itself, of escaping from the hardness and rawness of everyday surroundings into an idealized picture of civilized refinement, of believing that the essence of beauty must lie in what James Russell Lowell read about in Keats rather than what Walt Whitman saw in the streets of Brooklyn. The inescapable result of this is to make art an adornment rather than an organic expression of life, to confuse it with politeness and delicacy.[37]

This was indeed what Santayana had tried to convey, and his writings on the genteel tradition stand as a vivid reminder of the divergent tendencies within the American mind and of the dangers that attend their seemingly inexorable presence.

[37] *Theodore Dreiser* ([New York]: William Sloane Associates, 1951), p. 62.

Young Sammy's First Wild Oats

This piece of light, occasional verse was first delivered before
the Harvard literary club, The Signet, in 1900. Though very
little known, it nonetheless represents the first version of Santayana's theory of the genteel tradition to see print. Its allegorical
contrast between Uncle Sam and Young Sammy clearly pre-
figures the notion of two American mentalities which is basic
to his most influential statement, "The Genteel Tradition in
American Philosophy." The subject of this poem—the dilemma
posed by America's conduct of the Spanish-American War—is
also a matter of some interest, for Santayana was a Spanish subject and, as the poem shows, found himself in an ambiguous
position. Not that he felt spite for America's hostile action toward Spain; his emotion at the collapse of the Spanish empire
in America, as he makes clear in his autobiography, was one of
relief. Rather, Santayana's response was directed toward the
anti-imperialist outcry of American intellectuals such as his
colleague William James and his fellow Harvard poet William
Vaughn Moody, the point of view represented in the poem by
Deacon Plaster. This response, comically rendered through the

remarks of Doctor Wise, corresponds rather closely to Santayana's theory of the American intellectual tradition as it was to be set forth in "The Genteel Tradition in American Philosophy," thereby suggesting that the basic formulation of the idea of the genteel tradition may have crystalized in Santayana's mind as he groped for perspective on the complex of issues surrounding the war. Lending credence to this suggestion is Santayana's vivid recollection, in the last chapter of *The Middle Span,* of an exchange between William James and George Herbert Palmer in 1898 which may have served as the inspiration for the poem.

This poem is reprinted as it originally appeared in *The Harvard Lampoon Supplement,* XL:4 (November 20, 1900). A slightly revised version, carrying the subtitle "Lines written before the Presidential election of 1900," was published in *A Hermit of Carmel and Other Verses* (New York: Charles Scribner's Sons, 1901).

Victorious friends around this table,
   moisten, pray, your husky throats,
While I read a little fable
   called "Young Sammy's First Wild Oats."

'Mid Uncle Sam's expanded acres
   there's an old, secluded glade
Where gray Puritans and Quakers
   still grow fervid in the shade;

And the same great elms and beeches
   that once graced the ancestral farm,
Bending to the old man's speeches,
   lend their words an echo's charm.

Laurel, clematis, and vine
   weave green trellises about,
And three maples and a pine
   shut the mucker-village out.

Yet the smoke of trade and battle
   cannot quite be banished hence,
And the air-line to Seattle
   whizzes just behind the fence.

As one day old Deacon Plaster
   hobbled to the wonted nook,
There was Doctor Wise, the pastor
   meekly sitting with his book.

"What has happened, Brother Deacon,
   that you look so hot and vexed?
Is it something I might speak on
   when I preach on Sabbath next?"

"Doctor Wise," replied the other
   as he wiped the sweat away,
" 'Tis a wicked sin, my brother,
   you should preach on every day.

"Cousin Sammy's gone a-tooting
   to the Creole County fair,
Where the very sun's polluting
   and there's fever in the air.

"He has picked up three young lasses,
　three mulattoes on the mart,
Who have offered him free passes
　to their fortune and their heart.

"One young woman he respected,
　vowed he only came to woo.
But his word may be neglected
　since he ravished the other two.

"In the Porto Rican billing
　and carousing, I allow
That the little minx was willing,
　though she may be sorry now.

"But what came of those embraces
　and that taint of nigger blood?
Now he looks on outraged faces
　and can laugh, defying God:

"He can stretch his hand, relieving,
　and strike down a cheated slave.
Oh! if Uncle Sam were living,
　this would bring him to his grave!"

Deacon Plaster ceased and, sighing,
　mopped the reeking of his brain.
Doctor Wise, before replying,
　put his goggles on again.

"Brother Plaster, to be candid,
    were I managing the farm,
I should do as the old man did—
    lying low and safe from harm,

"Shoot at poachers from the hedges
    if they ventured within range,
Just round out my acre's edges,
    grow and grow, but never change.

"I am old, and you are old, sir:
    old the thoughts we live among.
If the truth were to be told, sir,
    none of us was ever young.

"In the towns of sombre Britain—
    merry England turned about—
We were marked at birth and smitten
    whom the Lord had chosen out;

"Picked to found a pilgrim nation,
    far from men, estranged, remote,
With the desert for a station
    and the ocean for a moat;

"To rebuke by sober living
    in the dread of wrath to come,
Of the joys of this world's giving
    the abominable sum.

"Yet all passion's seeds came smuggled
    in our narrow pilgrim ark,
And, unwatered, grew and struggled,
    pushed for ages through the dark,

"And, when summer granted pardon,
    burst into the upper air,
Till that desert was a garden
    and that sea a thoroughfare.

"Thus the virtue we rely on
    melted 'neath the heathen sun,
And what should have been a Sion
    came to be this Babylon.

"Ignorant of ancient sorrow,
    with hot young blood in their veins,
Now the prophets of the morrow
    Ply the spur and hold the reins.

"Can we blame them? Rather blame us,—
    us, who uttered idle things.
Our false prophecies shall shame us,
    and our weak imaginings.

"Liberty! delicious sound!
    The world loved it, and is free.
But what's freedom? To be bound
    by a chance majority.

"Few are rich and many poor,
　though all minds show one dull hue.
Equality we don't secure,
　mediocrity we do.

"Ah! what dreams beguiled our youth!
　Brothers we had hoped to be;
But competition is the truth
　of what we called fraternity.

"Can we blame them we mistaught
　if now they seek another guide
And, since our wisdom comes to nought,
　take counsel of their proper pride?

"Nature beckons them, inviting
　to a deeper draught of fate,
And, the heart's desire inciting,
　can we stop and bid them wait?

"If old Uncle Sam were living,
　this, you say, should never be:
Ah! if Uncle Sam were living,
　he might weep, but he must see.

"Yet he died in time, believing
　in the gods that ruled his days.
We, alas! survive him, grieving
　under gods we will not praise.

"The keen pleasures of December
  mean the joys of April lost;
And shall rising suns remember
  all the dream worlds they have crossed?

"All things mortal have their season:
  nothing lives, forever young,
But renews its life by treason
  to the thing from which it sprung,

"And when man has reached immortal
  mansions, after toiling long,
Life deserts him at the portal,
  and he only lives in song.

"As for Sam, the son, I wonder
  if you know the fellow's heart:
There may yet be something under
  nobler than the outer part.

"When he told that señorita
  that he kissed and hugged her close
Like a brother, did he cheat her?
  Did he cheat himself? Who knows?

"That he liked her, that is certain;
  that he wronged her isn't true.
On his thoughts I draw the curtain:
  I don't know them, nor do you.

"In her maid, the facile Rica,
  we have quite another case.
Hardly did he go to seek her,
  when she rushed to his embrace.

"I confess it was improper,
  but all flesh, alas! is flesh.
Things had gone too far to drop her;
  each was in the other's mesh.

"But with that poor Filipina,
  when she shrank from his caress,
His contemptible demeanor
  isn't easy to express.

"First he bought her, then he kicked her;
  but the truth is, he was drunk,
For that day had crowned him victor,
  and a Spanish fleet was sunk.

"You perceive I do not spare him,
  nor am blinded to his motes
By the Christian love I bear him;
  yes: he's sowing his wild oats.

"But you can't deny him talent;
  once his instinct is awake,
He can play the part of gallant
  and of soldier and of rake.

"And it's something to have spirit
   though in rashness first expressed.
Give me good blood to inherit:
   time and trial do the rest.

"He's not Uncle Sam, the father,
   that prim, pompous, honest man,
Yankee, or Virginian, rather:
   Sammy's an American—

"Lavish, clever, loud, and pushing,
   loving bargains, loving strife,
Kind, rude, fearless-eyed, unblushing,
   not yet settled down in life.

"Send him forth; the world will mellow
   his bluff youth, or nothing can.
Nature made the hearty fellow,
   Life will make the gentleman.

"And if Cousin Sam is callow,
   it was we who did the harm,
Letting his young soul lie fallow—
   the one waste spot in the farm—

"Trained by sordid inventories
   to scorn all he couldn't buy,
Puffed with miserable glories
   Shouted at an empty sky,

"Fooled with cant of a past era,
    droned 'twixt dreamy lid and lid,
Till his God was a chimera
    and the living God was hid.

"Let him look up from his standard
    to the older stars of heaven,
Seaward by whose might, and landward,
    all the tribes of men are driven;

"By whom ancient hopes were blasted,
    ancient labors turned to dust;
Whence the little that has lasted
    borrows patience to be just:

"And beholding tribulation,
    seeing whither states are hurled,
Let him sign his declaration
    of dependence on the world."

Thus the Doctor's sermon ended;
    the old Deacon shook his head,
For his conscience was offended
    and his wits had lost the thread.

So have mine, but there's my fable:
    now, and when you cast your votes,
Be as lenient as you're able
    on "Young Sammy's First Wild Oats."

The Genteel Tradition in
American Philosophy

In 1911, Santayana taught in the summer school of the University of California at Berkeley. He had accepted the position, apparently, because he knew that he was leaving the country and he wanted, before he left, to see something of the vast American landscape, of California, and the Pacific Ocean. Before returning, he delivered an address before the Philosophical Union on August 25, an occasion which he welcomed as "particularly favorable" for saying something he had "long wanted to say." Three thousand miles from Boston and five months from the time of leaving the country for good, he unburdened himself at long last on a subject that he was either too diffident or too polite to raise publicly in New England—the genteel tradition. The title of this famous indictment, "The Genteel Tradition in American Philosophy," is misleading, for the real subject is not Philosophy but the dominant intellectual tradition in America and its effect on artistic and speculative enterprises. Reprinted two years later in his *Winds of Doctrine,* this essay and the concept of the genteel tradition that it set forth were to have a tremendous impact on the cultural reappraisal that increasingly occupied thinking America in the first quarter of the century.

"The Genteel Tradition in American Philosophy" is reprinted from the *University of California Chronicle*, XIII:4 (October 11, 1911). Its tone was slightly softened when it was revised for inclusion in *Winds of Doctrine: Studies in Contemporary Opinion* (New York: Charles Scribner's Sons, 1913).

Ladies and Gentlemen: The privilege of addressing you to-day is very welcome to me, not merely for the honor of it, which is great, nor for the pleasures of travel, which are many, when it is California that one is visiting for the first time, but also because there is something I have long wanted to say which this occasion seems particularly favorable for saying. America is still a young country, and this part of it is especially so; and it would have been nothing extraordinary if, in this young country, material preoccupations had altogether absorbed people's minds, and they had been too much engrossed in living to reflect upon life, or to have any philosophy. The opposite, however, is the case. Not only have you already found time to philosophize in California, as your society proves, but the eastern colonists from the very beginning were a sophisticated race. As much as in clearing the land and fighting the Indians they were occupied, as they expressed it, in wrestling with the Lord. The country was new, but the race was tried, chastened, and full of solemn memories. It was an old wine in new bottles; and America did not have to wait for its present universities, with their departments of academic philosophy, in order to possess a living philosophy,—to have a distinct vision of the universe and definite convictions about human destiny.

Now this situation is a singular and remarkable one, and has many consequences, not all of which are equally fortunate. America is a young country with an old mentality: it has enjoyed the advantages of a child carefully brought up, and thoroughly indoctrinated; it has been a wise child. But a wise child, an old head on young shoulders, always has a comic and an unpromising side. The wisdom is a little thin and verbal, not aware of its full meaning and grounds; and physical and emotional growth may be stunted by it, or even deranged. Or when the child is too vigorous for that, he will develop a fresh mentality of his own, out of his observations and actual instincts; and this fresh mentality will interfere with the traditional mentality, and tend to reduce it to something perfunctory, conventional, and perhaps secretly despised. A philosophy is not genuine unless it inspires and expresses the life of those who cherish it. I do not think the hereditary philosophy of America has done much to atrophy the natural activities of the inhabitants; the wise child has not missed the joys of youth or of manhood; but what has happened is that the hereditary philosophy has grown stale, and that the academic philosophy afterwards developed has caught the stale odor from it. America is not simply, as I said a moment ago, a young country with an old mentality: it is a country with two mentalities, one a survival of the beliefs and standards of the fathers, the other an expression of the instincts, practice, and discoveries of the younger generations. In all the higher things of the mind—in religion, in literature, in the moral emotions—it is the hereditary spirit that still prevails, so much so that Mr. Bernard Shaw finds that America is a hundred years behind the times. The truth is that that one-half of the American mind, that not occupied intensely in practical affairs, has remained, I will not say high-and-dry, but slightly becalmed; it has floated gently in the backwater, while, alongside, in invention and industry and social organization the other half of the mind was leaping down a sort of Niagara Rapids. This division may be found symbolized in American architecture: a neat reproduction of the colonial mansion—with some modern comforts introduced surreptitiously—stands beside the sky-scraper. The American Will inhabits the sky-scraper; the American Intellect inhabits the colonial mansion. The one is the sphere of the American man; the other, at least predominantly, of the American woman. The one is all aggressive enterprise; the other is all genteel tradition.

Now, with your permission, I should like to analyze more fully how this interesting situation has arisen, how it is qualified, and whither it tends. And in the first place we should remember what, precisely, that philosophy was which the first settlers brought with them into the country. In strictness there was more than one; but we may confine our attention to what I will call Calvinism, since it is on this that the current academic philosophy has been grafted. I do not mean exactly the Calvinism of Calvin, or even of Jonathan Edwards; for in their systems there was much that was not pure philosophy, but rather faith in the externals and history of revelation. Jewish and Christian revelation was interpreted by these men, however, in the spirit of a particular philosophy, which might have arisen under any sky, and been associated with any other religion as well as with Protestant Christianity. In fact, the philosophical principle of Calvinism appears also in the Koran, in Spinoza, and in Cardinal Newman; and persons with no very distinctive Christian belief, like Carlyle or like Professor Royce, may be nevertheless, philosophically, perfect Calvinists. Calvinism, taken in this sense, is an expression of the agonized conscience. It is a view of the world which an agonized conscience readily embraces, if it takes itself seriously, as, being agonized, of course it must. Calvinism, essentially, asserts three things: that sin exists, that sin is punished, and that it is beautiful that sin should exist to be punished. The heart of the Calvinist is therefore divided between tragic concern at his own miserable condition, and tragic exultation about the universe at large. He oscillates between a profound abasement and a paradoxical elation of the spirit. To be a Calvinist philosophically is to feel a fierce pleasure in the existence of misery, especially of one's own, in that this misery seems to manifest the fact that the Absolute is irresponsible or infinite or holy. Human nature, it feels, is totally depraved: to have the instincts and motives that we necessarily have is a great scandal, and we must suffer for it; but that scandal is requisite, since otherwise the serious importance of being as we ought to be would not have been vindicated. ✳

To those of us who have not an agonized conscience this system may seem fantastic and even unintelligible; yet it is logically and intently thought out from its emotional premises. It can take permanent possession of a deep mind here and there, and under certain conditions it can become epidemic. Imagine, for instance, a small nation with an intense vitality, but on the verge of ruin, ecstatic and distressful, having a strict and minute code of laws, that paint life in sharp and violent chiaroscuro, all pure righteousness and black abominations, and exaggerating the consequences of both perhaps to infinity. Such a people were the Jews after the exile, and again the early Protestants. If such a people is philosophical at all, it will not improbably be Calvinistic. Even in the early American communities many of these conditions were fulfilled. The nation was small and isolated; it lived under pressure and constant trial; it was acquainted with but a small range of goods and evils. Vigilance over conduct and an absolute demand for personal integrity were not merely traditional things, but things that practical sages, like Franklin and Washington, recommended to their countrymen, because they were virtues that justified themselves visibly by their fruits. But soon these happy results themselves helped to relax the pressure of external circumstances, and indirectly the pressure of the agonized conscience within. The nation became numerous; it ceased to be either ecstatic or distressful; the high social morality which on the whole it preserved took another color; people remained honest and helpful out of good sense and good will rather than out of scrupulous adherence to any fixed principles. They retained their instinct for order, and often created order with surprising quickness; but the sanctity of law, to be obeyed for its own sake, began to escape them; it seemed too unpractical a notion, and not quite serious. In fact, the second and native-born American mentality began to take shape. The sense of sin totally evaporated. Nature, in the words of Emerson, was all beauty and commodity; and while operating on it laboriously, and drawing quick returns, the American began to drink in inspiration from it aesthetically. At the same time, in so broad a continent, he had elbow-room. His neighbors helped more than they hindered him; he wished their number to increase. Good-will became the great American virtue; and a passion arose for counting heads, and square miles, and cubic feet, and minutes saved—as if there had been anything to save them for. How strange to the American now that saying of Jonathan

Edwards, that men are naturally God's enemies! Yet that is an axiom to any intelligent Calvinist, though the words he uses may be different. If you told the modern American that he is totally depraved, he would think you were joking, as he himself usually is. He is convinced that he always has been, and always will be, victorious and blameless.

Calvinism thus lost its basis in American life. Some emotional natures, indeed, reverted in their religious revivals or private searchings of heart to the sources of the tradition; for any of the radical points of view in philosophy may cease to be prevalent, but none can cease to be possible. Other natures, more sensitive to the moral and literary influences of the world, preferred to abandon parts of their philosophy, hoping thus to reduce the distance which should separate the remainder from real life.

Meantime, if anybody arose with a special sensibility or a technical genius, he was in great straits; not being fed sufficiently by the world, he was driven in upon his own resources. The three American writers whose personal endowment was perhaps the finest—Poe, Hawthorne, and Emerson—had all a certain starved and abstract quality. They could not retail the genteel tradition; they were too keen, too perceptive, and too independent for that. But life offered them little digestible material, nor were they naturally voracious. They were fastidious, and under the circumstances they were starved. Emerson, to be sure, fed on books. There was a great catholicity in his reading; and he showed a fine tact in his comments, and in his way of appropriating what he read. But he read transcendentally, not historically, to learn what he himself felt, not what others might have felt before him. And to feed on books, for a

philosopher or a poet, is still to starve. Books can help him
to acquire form, or to avoid pitfalls; they cannot supply him
with substance, if he is to have any. Therefore the genius of
Poe and Hawthorne, and even of Emerson, was employed
on a sort of inner play, or digestion of vacancy. It was a
refined labor, but it was in danger of being morbid, or
tinkling, or self-indulgent. It was a play of intra-mental
rhymes. Their mind was like an old music-box, full of
tender echoes and quaint fancies. These fancies expressed
their personal genius sincerely, as dreams may; but they
were arbitrary fancies in comparison with what a real observer would have said in the premises. Their manner, in a
word, was subjective. In their own persons they escaped
the mediocrity of the genteel tradition, but they supplied
nothing to supplant it in other minds. ✳

✳The churches, likewise, although they modified their spirit,
had no philosophy to offer save a selection or a new emphasis on parts of what Calvinism contained. The theology
of Calvin, we must remember, had much in it besides philosophical Calvinism. A Christian tenderness, and a hope of
grace for the individual, came to mitigate its sardonic optimism; and it was these evangelical elements that the
Calvinistic churches now emphasized, seldom and with
blushes referring to hell-fire or infant damnation. Yet philosophic Calvinism, with a theory of life that would perfectly
justify hell-fire and infant damnation if they happened to
exist, still dominates the traditional metaphysics. It is an
ingredient, and the decisive ingredient, in what calls itself
idealism. But in order to see just what part Calvinism plays
in current idealism, it will be necessary to distinguish the
other chief element in that complex system, namely, transcendentalism. ✳

⋇Transcendentalism is the philosophy which the romantic era produced in Germany, and independently, I believe, in America also. Transcendentalism proper, like romanticism, is not any particular set of dogmas about what things exist; it is not a system of the universe regarded as a fact, or as a collection of facts. It is a method, a point of view, from which any world, no matter what it might contain, could be approached by a self-conscious observer. Transcendentalism is a systematic subjectivism. It studies the perspectives of knowledge, as they radiate from the self; it is a plan of those avenues of inference by which our ideas of things must be reached, if they are to afford any systematic or distant vistas. In other words, transcendentalism is the critical logic of science. Knowledge, it says, has a station, as in a watch-tower; it is always seated here and now, in the self of the moment. The past and the future, things inferred and things conceived, lie around it, painted as upon a panorama. They cannot be lighted up save by some centrifugal ray of the mind. ⋇

This is hardly the occasion for developing or explaining this delicate insight; suffice it to say, lest you should think later that I disparage transcendentalism, that as a method I regard it as correct and, when once suggested, unforgettable. I regard it as the chief contribution made in modern times to speculation. But it is a method only, an attitude we may always assume if we like and that will always be legitimate. It is no answer, and involves no particular answer, to the question: What exists; in what order is what exists produced; what is to exist in the future? This question must be answered by observing the object, and tracing humbly the movement of the object. It cannot be answered at all by harping on the fact that this object, if discovered, must be discovered by somebody, and by somebody who has an interest in discovering it. Yet the Germans who first gained the full transcendental insight were romantic people; they were more or less frankly poets; they were colossal egotists, and wished to make not only their own knowledge but the whole universe center about themselves. And full as they were of their romantic isolation and romantic liberty, it occurred to them to imagine that all reality might be a transcendental self and a romantic dreamer like themselves; nay, that it might be just their own transcendental self and their own romantic dreams extended indefinitely. Trancendental logic, the method of discovery for the mind, was to become also the method of evolution in nature and history. Transcendental method, so abused, produced transcendental myth. A conscientious critique of knowledge was turned into a sham system of nature. We must therefore distinguish sharply the transcendental grammar of the intellect, which is significant and potentially correct, from the various transcendental systems of the universe, which are chimeras.

In both its parts, however, transcendentalism had much to recommend it to American philosophers, for the transcendental method appealed to the individualistic and revolutionary temper of their youth, while transcendental myths enabled them to find a new status for their inherited theology, and to give what parts of it they cared to preserve some semblance of philosophical backing. This last was the use to which the transcendental method was put by Kant himself, who first brought it into vogue, before the terrible weapon had got out of hand, and became the instrument of pure romanticism. Kant came, he himself said, to remove knowledge in order to make room for faith, which in his case meant faith in Calvinism. In other words, he applied the transcendental method to matters of fact, reducing them thereby to human ideas, in order to give to the Calvinistic postulates of conscience a metaphysical validity. For Kant had a genteel tradition of his own, which he wished to remove to a place of safety, feeling that the empirical world had become too hot for it; and this place of safety was the region of transcendental myth. I need hardly say how perfectly this expedient suited the needs of philosophers in America, and it is no accident if the influence of Kant soon became dominant here. To embrace this philosophy was regarded as a sign of profound metaphysical insight, although the most mediocre minds found no difficulty in embracing it. In truth it was a sign of having been brought up in the genteel tradition, of feeling it weak, and of wishing to save it.

But the transcendental method, in its way, was also sympathetic to the American mind. It embodied, in a radical form, the spirit of Protestantism as distinguished from its inherited doctrines; it was autonomous, undismayed, calmly revolutionary; it felt that Will was deeper than Intellect; it focused everything here and now, and asked all things to show their credentials at the bar of the young self, and to prove their value for this latest born moment. These things are truly American; they would be characteristic of any young society with a keen and discursive intelligence, and they are strikingly exemplified in the thought and in the person of Emerson. They constitute what he called self-trust. Self-trust, like other transcendental attitudes, may be expressed in metaphysical fables. The romantic spirit may imagine itself to be an absolute force, evoking and molding the plastic world to express its varying moods. But for a pioneer who is actually a world-builder this metaphysical

47-51 - analysis of Emerson

illusion has a partial warrant in historical fact; far more warrant than it could boast of in the fixed and articulated society of Europe, among the moonstruck rebels and sulking poets of the romantic era. Emerson was a shrewd Yankee, by instinct on the winning side; he was a cheery, child-like soul, impervious to the evidence of evil, as of everything that it did not suit his transcendental individuality to appreciate or to notice. More, perhaps, than anybody that has ever lived, he practiced the transcendental method in all its purity. He had no system. He opened his eyes on the world every morning with a fresh sincerity, marking how things seemed to him then, or what they suggested to his spontaneous fancy. This fancy, for being spontaneous, was not always novel; it was guided by the habits and training of his mind, which were those of a preacher. Yet he never insisted on his notions so as to turn them into settled dogmas; he felt in his bones that they were myths. Sometimes, indeed, the bad example of other transcendentalists, less true than he to their method, or the pressing questions of unintelligent people, or the instinct we all have to think our ideas final, led him to the very verge of system-making; but he stopped short. Had he made a system out of his notion of compensation, or the over-soul, or spiritual laws, the result would have been as thin and forced as it is in other transcendental systems. But he coveted truth; and he returned to experience, to history, to poetry, to the natural science of his day, for new starting-points and hints toward fresh transcendental musings.

To covet truth is a very distinguished passion. Every philosopher says he is pursuing the truth, but this is seldom the case. As Mr. Bertrand Russell has observed, one reason why philosophers often fail to reach the truth is that often they do not desire to reach it. Those who are genuinely con-

cerned in discovering what happens to be true are rather
the men of science, the naturalists, the historians; and ordi-
narily they discover it, according to their lights. The truths
they find are never complete, and are not always important;
but they are integral parts of the truth, facts and circumstances that help to fill in the picture, and that no later
interpretation can invalidate or afford to contradict. But
professional philosophers are usually only scholastics: that
is, they are absorbed in defending some vested illusion or
some eloquent idea. Like lawyers or detectives, they study
the case for which they are retained, to see how much evidence or semblance of evidence they can gather for the defense, and how much prejudice they can raise against the
witnesses for the prosecution; for they know they are defending prisoners suspected by the world, and perhaps by
their own good sense, of falsification. They do not covet
truth, but victory and the dispelling of their own doubts.
What they defend is some system, that is, some view about
the totality of things, of which men are actually ignorant.
No system would ever have been framed if people had been
simply interested in knowing what is true, whatever it may
be. What produces systems is the interest in maintaining
against all comers that some favorite or inherited idea of
ours is sufficient and right. A system may contain an account
of many things which, in detail, are true enough; but as a
system, covering infinite possibilities that neither our experience nor our logic can prejudge, it must be a work of
imagination, and a piece of human soliloquy. It may be expressive of human experience, it may be poetical; but how
should any one who really coveted truth suppose that it
was true?

Emerson had no system; and his coveting truth had another
exceptional consequence: he was detached, unworldly, con-

templative. When he came out of the conventicle or the reform meeting, or out of the rapturous close atmosphere of the lecture-room, he heard nature whispering to him: "Why so hot, little sir?" No doubt the spirit or energy of the world is what is acting in us, as the sea is what rises in every little wave; but it passes through us, and cry out as we may, it will move on. Our privilege is to have perceived it as it moves. Our dignity is not in what we do, but in what we understand. The whole world is doing things. We are turning in that vortex; yet within us is silent observation, the speculative eye before which all passes, which bridges the distances and compares the combatants. On this side of his genius Emerson broke away from all conditions of age or country and represented nothing except intelligence itself.

There was another element in Emerson, curiously combined with transcendentalism, namely, his love and respect for Nature. Nature, for the transcendentalist, is precious because it is his own work, a mirror in which he looks at himself and says (like a poet relishing his own verses), "What a genius I am! Who would have thought there was such stuff in me?" And the philosophical egotist finds in his doctrine a ready explanation of whatever beauty and commodity nature actually has. No wonder, he says to himself, that nature is sympathetic, since I made it. And such a view, one-sided and even fatuous as it may be, undoubtedly sharpens the vision of a poet and a moralist to all that is inspiriting and symbolic in the natural world. Emerson was particularly ingenious and clear-sighted in feeling the spiritual uses of fellowship with the elements. This is something in which all Teutonic poetry is rich and which forms, I think, the most genuine and spontaneous part of modern taste, and especially of American taste. Just as some people are naturally enthralled and refreshed by music, so others are by landscape. Music and landscape make up the spiritual resources of those who cannot or dare not express their unfulfilled ideals in words. Serious poetry, profound religion (Calvinism, for instance) are the joys of an unhappiness that confesses itself; but when a genteel tradition forbids people to confess that they are unhappy, serious poetry and profound religion are closed to them by that; and since human life, in its depths, cannot then express itself openly, imagination is driven for comfort into abstract arts, where human circumstances are lost sight of, and human problems dissolve in a purer medium. The pressure of care is thus relieved, without its quietus being found in intelligence. To understand oneself is the classic form of consolation; to elude oneself is the romantic. In the presence of music or landscape human experience eludes itself; and thus romanticism is the bond between transcendental and naturalistic sentiment.

Have there been, we may ask, any successful efforts to escape from the genteel tradition, and to express something worth expressing behind its back? This might well not have occurred as yet; but America is so precocious, it has been trained by the genteel tradition to be so wise for its years, that some indications of a truly native philosophy and poetry are already to be found. I might mention the humorists, of whom you here in California have had your share. The humorists, however, only half escape the genteel tradition; their humor would lose its savor if they had wholly escaped it. They point to what contradicts it in the facts; but not in order to abandon the genteel tradition, for they have nothing solid to put in its place. When they point out how ill many facts fit into it, they do not clearly conceive that this militates against the standard, but think it a funny perversity in the facts. Of course, did they earnestly respect the genteel tradition, such an incongruity would seem to them sad, rather than ludicrous. Perhaps the prevalence of humor in America, in and out of season, may be taken as one more evidence that the genteel tradition is present pervasively, but everywhere weak. Similarly in Italy, during the Renaissance, the Catholic tradition could not be banished from the intellect, since there was nothing articulate to take its place; yet its hold on the heart was singularly relaxed. The consequence was that humorists could regale themselves with the foibles of monks and of cardinals, with the credulity of fools, and the bogus miracles of the saints; not intending to deny the theory of the church, but caring for it so little at heart, that they could find it infinitely amusing that it should be contradicted in men's lives, and that no harm should come of it. So when Mark Twain says, "I was born of poor but dishonest parents," the humor depends on the parody of the genteel Anglo-Saxon convention that it is disreputable to be poor; but to hint at the hollowness of it would not be amusing if it did not remain at bottom one's habitual conviction.

The one American writer who has left the genteel tradition entirely behind is perhaps Walt Whitman. For this reason educated Americans find him rather an unpalatable person, who they sincerely protest ought not to be taken for a representative of their culture; and he certainly should not, because their culture is so genteel and traditional. But the foreigner may sometimes think otherwise, since he is looking for what may have arisen in America to express, not the polite and conventional American mind, but the spirit and the inarticulate principles that animate the community, on which its own genteel mentality seems to sit rather lightly.

When the foreigner opens the pages of Walt Whitman, he thinks that he has come at last upon something representative and original. In Walt Whitman democracy is carried into psychology and morals. The various sights, moods, and emotions are given each one vote; they are declared to be all free and equal, and the innumerable common-place moments of life are suffered to speak like the others. Those moments formerly reputed great are not excluded, but they are made to march in the ranks with their companions,— plain foot-soldiers and servants of the hour. Nor does the refusal to discriminate stop there; we must carry our principle further down, to the animals, to inanimate nature, to the cosmos as a whole. Whitman became a pantheist; but his pantheism, unlike that of the Stoics and of Spinoza, was unintellectual, lazy, and self-indulgent; for he simply felt jovially that everything real was good enough, and that he was good enough himself. In him Bohemia rebelled against the genteel tradition; but the reconstruction that alone can justify revolution did not ensue. His attitude, in principle, was utterly disintegrating; his poetic genius fell back to the lowest level, perhaps, to which it is possible for poetic genius to fall. He reduced his imagination to a passive sensorium for the registering of impressions. No element of construction remained in it, and therefore no element of penetration. But his scope was wide; and his lazy, desultory apprehension was poetical. His work, for the very reason that it is so rudimentary, contains a beginning, or rather many beginnings, that might possibly grow into a noble moral imagination, a worthy filling for the human mind. An American in the nineteenth century who completely disregarded the genteel tradition could hardly have done more.

But there is another distinguished man, lately lost to this country, who has given some rude shocks to this tradition and who, as much as Whitman, may be regarded as representing the genuine, the long silent American mind—I mean William James. He and his brother Henry were as tightly swaddled in the genteel tradition as any infant geniuses could be, for they were born in Cambridge, and in a Swedenborgian household. Yet they burst those bands almost entirely. The ways in which the two brothers freed themselves, however, are interestingly different. Mr. Henry James has done it by adopting the point of view of the outer world, and by turning the genteel American tradition, as he turns everything else, into a subject-matter for analysis.

For him it is a curious habit of mind, intimately comprehended, to be compared with other habits of mind, also well known to him. Thus he has overcome the genteel tradition in the classic way, by understanding it. With William James too this infusion of worldly insight and European sympathies was a potent influence, especially in his earlier days; but the chief source of his liberty was another. It was his personal spontaneity, similar to that of Emerson, and his personal vitality, similar to that of nobody else. Convictions and ideas came to him, so to speak, from the subsoil. He had a prophetic sympathy with the dawning sentiments of the age, with the moods of the dumb majority. His scattered words caught fire in many parts of the world. His way of thinking and feeling represented the true America, and represented in a measure the whole ultra-modern, radical world. Thus he eluded the genteel tradition in the romantic way, by continuing it into its opposite. The romantic mind, glorified in Hegel's dialectic (which is not dialectic at all, but a sort of tragi-comic history of experience), is always rendering its thoughts unrecognizable through the infusion of new insights, and through the insensible transformation of the moral feeling that accompanies them, till at last it has completely reversed its old judgments under cover of expanding them. Thus the genteel tradition was led a merry dance when it fell again into the hands of a genuine and vigorous romanticist, like William James. He restored their revolutionary force to its neutralized elements, by picking them out afresh, and emphasizing them separately, according to his personal predilections.

For one thing, William James kept his mind and heart wide open to all that might seem, to polite minds, odd, personal, or visionary in religion and philosophy. He gave a sincerely respectful hearing to sentimentalists, mystics, spiritualists, wizards, cranks, quacks, and impostors—for it is hard to draw the line, and James was not willing to draw it prematurely. He thought, with his usual modesty, that any of these might have something to teach him. The lame, the halt, the blind, and those speaking with tongues could come to him with the certainty of finding sympathy; and if they were not healed, at least they were comforted, that a famous professor should take them so seriously; and they began to feel that after all to have only one leg, or one hand, or one eye, or to have three, might be in itself no less beauteous than to have just two, like the stolid majority. Thus William James became the friend and helper of those groping, nervous, half-educated, spiritually disinherited, emotionally hungry individuals of which America is full. He became, at the same time, their spokesman and representative before the learned world; and he made it a chief part of his vocation to recast what the learned world has to offer, so that as far as possible it might serve the needs and interests of these people.

Yet the normal practical masculine American, too, had a friend in William James. There is a feeling abroad now, to which biology and Darwinism lend some color, that theory is simply an instrument for practice, and intelligence merely a help toward material survival. Bears, it is said, have fur and claws, but poor naked man is condemned to be intelligent, or he will perish. This feeling William James embodied in that theory of thought and of truth which he called pragmatism. Intelligence, he thought, is no miraculous, idle faculty, by which we mirror passively any or every thing that happens to be true, reduplicating the real world to no purpose. Intelligence has its roots and its issue in the context of events; it is one kind of practical adjustment, an experimental act, a form of vital tension. It does not essentially serve to picture other parts of reality, but to connect them. This view was not worked out by William James in its psychological and historical details; unfortunately he developed it chiefly in controversy against its opposite, which he called intellectualism, and which he hated with all the hatred of which his kind heart was capable. Intellectualism, as he conceived it, was pure pedantry; it impoverished and verbalized everything, and tied up nature in red tape. Ideas and rules that may have been occasionally useful, it put in the place of the full-blooded irrational movement of life which had called them into being; and these abstractions, so soon obsolete, it strove to fix and to worship forever. Thus all creeds and theories and all formal precepts sink in the estimation of the pragmatist to a local and temporary grammar of action; a grammar that must be changed slowly by time, and may be changed quickly by genius. To know things as a whole, or as they are eternally, if there is anything eternal in them, is not only beyond our powers, but would prove worthless, and perhaps even fatal to our lives. Ideas are not mirrors, they are weapons; their function is to prepare us to meet events, as future experience may unroll them. Those ideas that disappoint us are false ideas; those to which events are true are true themselves.

This may seem a very utilitarian view of the mind; and I confess I think it a partial one, since the logical force of beliefs and ideas, their truth or falsehood as assertions, has been overlooked altogether, or confused with the vital force of the material processes which these ideas express. It is an external view only, which marks the place and conditions of the mind in nature, but neglects its specific essence; as if a jewel were defined as a round hole in a ring. Nevertheless, the more materialistically we interpret the pragmatist theory of what the mind is, the more vitalistic our theory of nature will have to become. If the intellect is a device produced in organic bodies to expedite their processes, these organic bodies must have interests and a chosen direction in their life; otherwise their life could not be expedited, nor could anything be useful to it. In other words—and this is a third point at which the philosophy of William James has played havoc with the genteel tradition, while ostensibly defending it—nature must be conceived anthropomorphically and in psychological terms. Its purposes are not to be static harmonies, self-unfolding destinies, the logic of spirit, the spirit of logic, or any other formal method and abstract law; its purposes are to be concrete endeavors, finite efforts of souls living in an environment which they transform and by which they, too, are affected. A spirit, the divine spirit as much as the human, as this new animism conceives it, is a romantic adventurer. Its future is undetermined. Its scope, its duration, and the quality of its life, are all contingent. This spirit grows; it buds and sends forth feelers, sounding the depths around for such other centers of force or life as may exist there. It has a vital momentum, but no predetermined goal. It uses its past as a stepping-stone, or rather as a diving-board, but has an absolutely fresh will at each moment to plunge this way or that into the unknown. The universe is an experiment; it is unfinished. It has no ultimate or total nature, because it has no end. It embodies no formula or statable law; any formula is at best a poor abstraction, describing what, in some region and for some time, may be the most striking characteristic of existence; the law is a description *a posteriori* of the habit things have chosen to acquire, and which they may possibly throw off altogether. What a day may bring forth is uncertain; uncertain even to God. Omniscience is impossible; time is real; what had been omniscience hitherto might discover something more to-day. "There shall be news," William James was fond of saying with rapture, quoting from the unpublished poem of an obscure friend, "there shall be news in heaven!" There is almost certainly, he thought, a God now; there may be several gods, who might exist together, or one after the other. We might, by our conspiring sympathies, help to make a new one. Much in us is doubtless immortal; we survive death for some time in a recognizable form; but what our career and transformations may be in the sequel, we cannot tell, although we may help to determine them by our daily choices. Observation must be continual, if our ideas are to remain true. Eternal vigilance is the price of knowledge; perpetual hazard, perpetual experiment keep quick the edge of life.

This is, so far as I know, a new philosophical vista; it is a conception never before presented, although implied, perhaps, in various quarters, as in Norse and even Greek mythology. It is a vision radically empirical and radically romantic; and as William James himself used to say, the vision and not the arguments of a philosopher is the interesting and influential thing about him. William James, rather too generously, attributed this vision to M. Bergson, and regarded him in consequence as a philosopher of the first rank, whose thought was to be one of the turning-points in history. M. Bergson had killed intellectualism. It was his book on creative evolution, said James with humorous emphasis, that had come at last to *"écraser l'infâme."* We may suspect, notwithstanding, that intellectualism, infamous and crushed, will survive the blow; and if the author of the Book of Ecclesiastes were now alive, and heard that there shall be news in heaven, he would doubtless say that there may possibly be news there, but that under the sun there is nothing new—not even radical empiricism or radical romanticism, which from the beginning of the world has been the philosophy of those who as yet had had little experience; for to the blinking little child it is not merely something in the world that is new daily, but everything is new all day.

I am not concerned with the rights and wrongs of that controversy; my point is only that William James, in this genial evolutionary view of the world, has given a rude shock to the genteel tradition. What! The world a gradual improvization? Creation unpremeditated? God a sort of young poet or struggling artist? William James is an advocate of theism; pragmatism adds one to the evidences of religion; that is excellent. But is not the cool abstract piety of the genteel getting more than it asks for? This empirical naturalistic God is too crude and positive a force; he will work miracles, he will answer prayers, he may inhabit distinct places, and have distinct conditions under which alone he can operate; he is a neighboring being, whom we can act upon, and rely upon for specific aids, as upon a personal friend, or a physician, or an insurance company. How disconcerting! Is not this new theology a little like superstition? And yet how interesting, how exciting, if it should happen to be true! I am far from wishing to suggest that such a view seems to me more probable than conventional idealism or than Christian orthodoxy. All three are in the region of dramatic system-making and myth, to which probabilities are irrelevant. If one man says the moon is sister to the sun, and another that she is his daughter, the question is not which notion is more probable, but whether either of them is at all expressive. The so-called evidences are devised afterwards, when faith and imagination have prejudged the issue. The force of William James's new theology, or romantic cosmology, lies only in this: that it has broken the spell of the genteel tradition, and enticed faith in a new direction, which on second thoughts may prove no less alluring than the old. The important fact is not that the new fancy might possibly be true—who shall know that?—but that it has entered the heart of a leading American to conceive and to cherish it. The genteel tradition cannot be dislodged by these insurrections; there are circles to which it is still congenial, and where it will be preserved. But it has been challenged and (what is perhaps more insidious) it has been discovered. No one need be brow-beaten any longer into accepting it. No one need be afraid, for instance, that his fate is sealed because some young prig may call him a dualist; the pint would call the quart a dualist, if you tried to pour the quart into him. We need not be afraid of being less profound, for being direct and sincere. The intellectual world may be traversed in many directions; the whole has not been surveyed; there is a great career in it open to talent. That is a sort of knell, that tolls the passing of the genteel tradition. Something else is now in the field; something else can appeal to the imagination, and be a thousand times more idealistic than academic idealism, which is often simply a way of white-washing and adoring things as they are. The illegitimate monopoly which the genteel tradition had established over what ought to be assumed and what ought to be hoped for has been broken down by the first-born of the family, by the genius of the race. Henceforth there can hardly be the same peace and the same pleasure in hugging the old proprieties. Hegel will be to the next generation what Sir William Hamilton was to the last. Nothing will have been disproved, but everything will have been abandoned. An honest man has spoken, and the cant of the genteel tradition has become harder for young lips to repeat.

With this I have finished such a sketch as I am here able to offer you of the genteel tradition in American philosophy. The subject is complex, and calls for many an excursus and qualifying footnote; yet I think the main outlines are clear enough. The chief fountains of this tradition were Calvinism and transcendentalism. Both were living fountains; but to keep them alive they required, one an agonized conscience, and the other a radical subjective criticism of knowledge. When these rare metaphysical preoccupations disappeared—and the American atmosphere is not favorable to either of them—the two systems ceased to be inwardly understood; they subsisted as sacred mysteries only; and the combination of the two in some transcendental system of the universe (a contradiction in principle) was doubly artificial. Besides, it could hardly be held with a single mind. Natural science, history, the beliefs implied in labor and invention, could not be disregarded altogether; so that the transcendental philosopher was condemned to a double allegiance, and to not letting his left hand know the bluff that his right hand was putting up. Nevertheless, the difficulty in bringing practical inarticulate convictions to expression is very great, and the genteel tradition has subsisted in the academic mind, for want of anything equally academic to take its place.

The academic mind, however, has had its flanks turned. On the one side came the revolt of the Bohemian temperament, with its poetry of crude naturalism; on the other side came an impassioned empiricism, welcoming popular religious witnesses to the unseen, reducing science to an instrument of success in action, and declaring the universe to be wild and young, and not to be harnessed by the logic of any school.

This revolution, I should think, might well find an echo among you, who live in a thriving society, and in the presence of a virgin and prodigious world. When you transform nature to your uses, when you experiment with her forces, and reduce them to industrial agents, you cannot feel that nature was made by you or for you, for then these adjustments would have been preestablished. You must feel, rather, that you are an offshoot of her life; one brave little force among her immense forces. When you escape, as you love to do, to your forests and your Sierras, I am sure again that you do not feel you made them, or that they were made for you. They have grown, as you have grown, only more massively and more slowly. In their non-human beauty and peace they stir the sub-human depths and the super-human possibilities of your own spirit. It is no transcendental logic that they teach; and they give no sign of any deliberate morality seated in the world. It is rather the vanity and superficiality of all logic, the needlessness of argument, the finitude of morals, the strength of time, the fertility of matter, the variety, the unspeakable variety, of possible life. Everything is measurable and conditioned, indefinitely repeated, yet in repetition, twisted somewhat from its old form. Everywhere is beauty and nowhere permanence, everywhere an incipient harmony nowhere an intention, nor a responsibility, nor a plan. It is the irresistible suasion of this daily spectacle, it is the daily discipline of contact with things, so different from the verbal discipline of the schools, that will, I trust, inspire the philosophy of your children. A Californian whom I had recently the pleasure of meeting observed that, if the philosophers had lived among your mountains their systems would have been different from what they are. Certainly, I should say, very different from what those systems are from which the European genteel tradition has handed down since Socrates; for these systems are egotistical; directly or indirectly they are anthropocentric, and inspired by the conceited notion that man, or human reason, or the human distinction between good and evil, is the center and pivot of the universe. That is what the mountains and the woods should make you at last ashamed to assert. From what, indeed, does the society of nature liberate you, that you find it so sweet? It is hardly (is it?) that you wish to forget your past, or your friends, or that you have any secret contempt for your present ambitions. You respect these, you respect them perhaps too much; you are not suffered by the genteel tradition to criticize or to reform them at all radically. No; it is the yoke of this genteel tradition itself, your tyrant from the cradle to the grave, that these primeval solitudes lift from your shoulders. They suspend your forced sense of your own importance not merely as individuals, but even as men.

They allow you, in one happy moment, at once to play and to worship, to take yourselves simply, humbly, for what you are, and to salute the wild, indifferent, noncensorious infinity of nature. You are admonished that what you can do avails little materially, and in the end nothing. At the same time, through wonder and pleasure, you are taught speculation. You learn what you are really fitted to do, and where lie your natural dignity and joy, namely, in representing many things, without being them, and in letting your imagination, through sympathy, celebrate and echo their life. Because the peculiarity of man is that his machinery for reaction on external things has involved an imaginative transcript of these things, which is preserved and suspended in his fancy; and the interest and beauty of this inward landscape, rather than any fortunes that may await his body in the outer world, constitute his proper happiness. By their mind, its scope, quality, and temper, we estimate men, for by the mind only do we exist as men, and are more than so many storage-batteries for material energy. Let us therefore be frankly human. Let us be content to live in the mind.

Shakespeare: Made in America

This brief essay, one of over a dozen Santayana was to contribute to the *New Republic* during its first two years of publication, is admittedly little more than a playful exercise and is not aimed directly at the genteel tradition. Yet it reveals his attitude towards two aspects of American culture that significantly shaped his theory of the genteel tradition: the impoverishment of America's cultural heritage, and the inherent effect of that impoverishment on American poetry and poetic sensibility. This was not merely a casual concern, for Santayana had not taken lightly the failure of his career as a poet and the failure of the "Harvard poets" generally. He persisted in thinking that the cause of this failure was in large part a matter of the environment or, as he put it, "the lack of air to breathe." This stifling atmosphere, he believed, was directly attributable to the genteel intellectual climate. If Santayana had any personal scores to settle with the genteel tradition, this was one of the most important. "Shakespeare: Made in America" may be profitably read in that light.

This essay first appeared in the *New Republic,* II:17 (February 27, 1915) and was reprinted in the *New Republic Anthology 1915:1935,* ed. Groff Conklin (New York: Dodge Publishing Company, [1936]).

Custom blinds us to the costume of thought. Not until the fashion has entirely changed do we see how extravagant the old costume was. The late middle ages and the renaissance, when modern languages took shape, had a very elaborate and modish dress for the mind as well as for the body. Notice, for instance, how Shakespeare can deck out a Hock sentiment, proper to any schoolboy:

> When in disgrace with fortune and men's eyes
> I all alone beweep my outcast state
> And trouble deaf heaven with my bootless cries
> And look upon myself and curse my fate,
> Wishing me like to one more rich in hope,
> Featur'd like him, like him with friends possess'd,
> Desiring this man's art and that man's scope,
> With what I most enjoy contented least,
> Yet in these thoughts myself almost despising,—
> Haply I think on thee; and then my state,
> Like to the lark at break of day arising
> From sullen earth, sings hymns at heaven's gate:
> For thy sweet love remember'd such wealth brings
> That then I scorn to change my state with kings.

[handwritten margin notes: "self-doubt", "envy", "solace in a lour"]

For Shakespeare this sonnet is comparatively plain and direct, yet it is simply encrusted with old-fashioned jewels and embroideries. How much so will become clear if we venture to paraphrase it, scrupulously leaving out every suggestion that could not have had its origin in the twentieth century and in America.

In the first few lines almost every connotation is obsolete and will have to be abandoned. So the idea of falling out of favor at a court where the capricious monarch is Fortune. This mythological Fortune was rather a verbal deity from the beginning and had become merely rhetorical even in Shakespeare's time; for us it is worse, and the unrepublican image is inadmissible. To *beweep* anything is also contrary to our manners; if tears ever escape us it is not ceremoniously nor as a fit accompaniment to magnificent lamentations. As to *men's eyes*, we look through our eyes, but seldom talk through them; and if we wish to shake off an objectionable friend we do not cast withering glances upon him, like the noble savage. We simply avoid the man; or if we are inclined to be offensively demonstrative, we cut him. The word *outcast* is still current; but the background which gave poignancy to that metaphor belongs to a bygone age. No one can be easily excommunicated in our tolerant society. If one circle disowns him he will slip into another, perhaps with relief, and find it no less self-respecting, even in jail; and if he makes bold to flaunt his crime or his heresy, he will excite more interest than loathing, and a party of sympathizers will probably flock to his side.

No less obsolete is the habit of troubling heaven with one's bootless cries. Even the lover in the sonnet, though he might have prayed, would hardly have emitted cries; only in remote antiquity his predecessors in the art of troubling heaven may actually have wailed. Nowadays hardly anybody would pray in the hope of recovering his friends or his property by divine interposition. People certainly have recourse to religion, and often in a more desperate need than ever; but to modern feeling religion opens a second

sphere of interest and hope, without being expected to
further our worldly hopes and interests.

In the body of the sonnet there are a number of phrases
which, without being in the least archaic, have a certain
grand sweeping air and *panache* about them quite foreign
to our experience. The word *art*, for instance, to most
Americans suggests the profession of painting; the intended
faculty of doing all things easily and well would have to
be called ability or skill, or more pungently and characteristically, *brains*. This single transition from art to brains
speaks volumes. Again, while no nation was ever more
hopeful than America or more optimistic, to say *rich in
hope* is to give the matter a different twist. You are optimistic when you take for granted or religiously assure yourself that the future, whatever it may be, will be all right,
and will somehow grow better and better. You are rich in
hope when you have great and definite expectations, are
heir or aspirant to an exalted position, and can picture in
a concrete form the happy future before you. So a bride-
groom is rich in hope on his wedding morning, or an ex-
pectant mother when making bibs for her first-born; but
the optimist may be as poor in hope as in experience.

Similarly the phrase *I look upon myself* expresses something
different from our self-consciousness. It describes the shock
of suddenly seeing yourself as others see you, as when you
unexpectedly come upon yourself in a mirror. The poet is
borrowing men's eyes in order to consider and pity himself;
he is not retreating into a psychological observation of what
is hidden from others in his consciousness.

The eleventh and twelfth lines will have to be sacrificed

in their entirety. There are no larks in America. There is no heaven in modern cosmology such that the blue sky in which larks sing should be called the gate of it. And what hymns could the poet have been thinking of? Christmas carols, perhaps, or such as the choir of Magdalen College in Oxford greet the sunrise with on May morning from the top of their lovely tower. In any case they were pre-Puritan hymns, hymns of joyful familiarity with a religion sweetly and humanly miraculous, hymns not associated with drawling tunes, funerals, or a vague sense of constraint and edification. For these two lines, therefore, we must substitute something wholly different, yet as nearly equivalent as possible. I can think of nothing domesticated in America nearer to larks and to bright religion than music is. So orchestral strains shall take the place of larks, with profound apologies; and in speaking of music we may perhaps slightly inflate the poetic bellows, since modern shyness does not attack our souls so much in that invisible wilderness.

As to the final couplet, we may still talk occasionally of being as happy as a king or as drunk as a lord, but whatever seduction there may once have been in those images, they have paled. Something of far greater moment, however, lies submerged here. The unsophisticated reader may pass approvingly over the phrase *thy sweet love,* as if the poet might just as well have written *our sweet love* instead, meaning that mutual, complete, hearty, happy, plebeian love which alone should figure in our revised American version. Yet as a matter of fact the sentiment and pathos of the original are profoundly different, being charged with the most exotic metaphysical overtones. If we compare this sonnet with the rest of Shakespeare's, and consider the

W. H. to whom at least by a poetic fiction they were addressed, it becomes evident that *thy sweet love* can only mean *the sweet love of thee,* a love which the poet did not and could not aspire to see returned. That ornate and exuberant age had so much passion to spare that it could think it but graceful adulation for a poet to address the intensest and richest effusions of love to some insipid youth in a high station. And behind that lavish play of expression (for perhaps it was nothing more) we must not ignore the possibility that the passion expressed may sometimes have been real, at least in those who first set this literary fashion; and in that case, seeing that even if graciously tolerated, such adoration could not possibly be mutual, we are at once transported into the dim sanctuary of Platonic love, where youth and beauty, at an aesthetic remove and because of their intrinsic virtue, are reputed to communicate a supreme and sufficient bliss to the worshipper, with all those moral and saving effects which this sonnet, for instance, celebrates. The lover is his infatuation, and in the religious chastening of it, is said somehow to find God. Humbug or philosophy, this Platonic mysticism has long been a classic refuge of hopeless emotion, and Shakespeare's sonnets march conventionally in the devout procession. Such ambiguous mysteries, however, are alien to modern sentiment and to the plain man's experience, and we may shut them out without further parlance.

Plucked of all its Elizabethan feathers, our sonnet might then present somewhat the following appearance:

> When times are hard and old friends fall away
> And all alone I lose my hope and pluck,
> Doubting if God can hear me when I pray,

And brood upon myself and curse my luck,
Envying some stranger for his handsome face,
His wit, his wealth, his chances, or his friends,
Desiring this man's brains and that man's place,
And vexed with all I have that makes amends,
Yet in these thoughts myself almost despising,—
By chance I think of you; and then my mind,
Like music from deep sullen murmurs rising
To peals and raptures, leaves the earth behind;
For if you care for me, what need I care
To own the world or be a millionaire?

The reader may laugh, but I have not made the sonnet absurd on purpose; on the contrary I have tried to keep it as good as possible under the conditions imposed. The experiment is not intended to show how an American poet would actually feel or treat Shakespeare's subject, for he would either compose fine imitative literature, with a lapse here and there which he might not be conscious of, or else he would give birth to something entirely novel. The experiment is meant only to make evident how much old finery there is in our literary baggage, and how original an original poet would have to be. Any wise man of Shakespeare's time might have prophesied that ruffs would no longer be worn in three hundred years, but only a genius could have foretold our trousers. So any critic may unfrock Shakespeare, but to dress his thought up again in the costume of a future poetry can be given only to the future poets themselves.

Genteel American Poetry

Another of the essays sent to the burgeoning *New Republic* while Santayana was trapped in England during World War I was this witty commentary on nineteenth-century American poetry. Here the genteel tradition's poetic product is laid out in the crisp epigrams that were the hallmark of Santayana's most spirited writing. But this brief essay is more than a collection of barbs; it proves to be, upon careful examination, an amazingly succinct and incisive analysis of nineteenth-century America's poetic malaise. As such it adds an important dimension to Santayana's increasingly comprehensive theory of the genteel tradition. The high humor of this essay, quite apart from the deftness of its characterizations, makes it one of the most delightful of Santayana's fugitive pieces.

"Genteel American Poetry" is reprinted from the *New Republic*, III:30 (May 29, 1915).

Poetry in America before the Civil War was an honest and adequate phenomenon. It spoke without affectation in a language and style which it could take for granted. It was candid in its tastes, even in that frank and gentle romanticism which attached it to Evangelines and Maud Mullers. It modulated in obvious ways the honorable conventions of the society in which it arose. It was a simple, sweet, humane, Protestant literature, grandmotherly in that sedate spectacled wonder with which it gazed at this terrible world and said how beautiful and how interesting it all was.

The accent of these poets was necessarily provincial, their outlook and reflectiveness were universal enough. Their poetry was indeed without sensuous beauty, splendor, passion, or volume, but so was the life it expressed. To be a really great poet an American at that time would have had to be a rebel.

It would have been an interesting thing if a thunderclap had suddenly broken that cloudless new-world haying-weather, and if a cry of exasperation had escaped some strong soul, surfeited by the emptiness and blandness of that prim little moral circle that thought it had overcome everything when in fact it had touched nothing. But to the genteel mind of America, before Walt Whitman and the Civil War, there was no self-respecting opposition. Of course, in that boundless field of convention, prosperity and mediocrity, a wild poppy might struggle up weedily here and there amid the serried corn. But the irregular genius had no chance. He felt sincerely ashamed of himself. He hid his independence, fled to the back woods or to Europe, and his sad case was hushed up as if it had been insanity (for insanity was hushed up too) and buried with a whisper under the vaguely terrible epitaph DISSIPATED. He

probably died young; at any rate he never "did" anything.
Whoever was unharnessed was lost.

In England at about the same time or earlier there was a
marked division between the poets who were national,
conventional and edifying and those who were disaffected.
Wordsworth and Tennyson were more than matched by
Byron, Shelley, and Swinburne. What occasioned this division in England was the very distinct and intolerant character of the national mind. You either identified yourself
with it and expressed it sympathetically, or you broke away
from it altogether, denounced it as narrow, stupid, and op-
pressive, and removed yourself offendedly to Greece or to
Italy, to sing of lovely sensuality or celestial justice. A cir-
cumstance that made such romantic truancy all the easier
for poets was the classical cast of their education. History,
religion, and literary tradition, united with the ease of
travel, carried the mind of every educated man continually
beyond the limits of his country and its present ways. When
one's moral possessions are so largely of foreign extraction,
it requires no break with one's education, but merely a
certain deepening and arrest in it, for things not national
to seem the right environment for the soul. Exile accordingly did not sterilize the British poets: on the contrary, it
seemed to liberate their genius and carry them back, across
the Reformation, to an England as poetical if not so vigorous as that of Shakespeare.

Why did no disaffected Americans figure among these
poets of the foreign, or rather of the human, ideal? The
provocation to secede was certainly not less than in England; for if the country was not dominated by any church
or aristocracy, it was dominated no less rigidly by democ-

racy and commercialism. The land was indeed broader, and those who felt spiritually restive could without any great scandal make for the wild West. That was certainly a resource for adventurous temperaments; but those whose impatience was moral, whose need was not so much for room as for something to fill it, could hardly be satisfied there; for morally all America even to-day is far more monotonous and uniform than England ever was. It was perhaps this very pressure of sameness which might have justified a poetic protest, that prevented it from arising.

The insurrection that actually took place was that of Walt Whitman, with the magnificent intention of being wholly direct, utterly sincere, and bothering about nothing that was not an experience of the soul and of the sense here in the motley foreground of life. It is notable that this powerful insurrection in favor of what is modern and national has made so little difference. Of course, nothing can compel people to read or to like an author that displeases them. Perhaps Walt Whitman made the mistake of supposing that what was vital in America was only what was absolutely modern and native, to the exclusion of anything that might have been transplanted to this country ready-made, like the Christian religion or the English language. He wished to be wholly impressionistic, wholly personal, wholly American, and the result was perhaps that he was simply mystical, missing the articulation of the great world, as well as the constructive mind of his own age and country. After all, the future often belongs to what has a past. Walt Whitman renounced old forms without achieving a new one, and in his thought also there was more detritus than invention.

At any rate, the genteel manner having become obsolete,

and the manner of the great mystical tramp not having taken root, the poetic mind of America suffered a certain dispersion. It was solicited in turn by the seductive aesthetic school, by the influence of Browning, with his historico-dramatic obsessions, by symbolism, by the desperate determination to be expressive even with nothing to express, and by the resolve to write poetry which is not verse, so as to be sure of not writing verse which is not poetry. The spontaneous me has certainly been beaten in the first round by the artistic ego. Meantime the average human genteel person, with a heart, a morality, and a religion, who is after all in the majority, is left for the moment without any poetry to give him pleasure or to do him honor.

The Moral Background

This essay stands first in *Character and Opinion in the United States,* the major part of which, as Santayana tells us in the preface, is "composed of lectures originally addressed to British audiences." The two essays that follow it in the present collection are earlier published versions of lectures that were revised and included in the volume, but "The Moral Background" does not seem to have appeared in print previously and may not have been given as a lecture. Although this strongly suggests that it was probably written later than the others, it is allowed to precede them here because its original purpose was, in part, to introduce and prepare for them, as well as for pieces not here included.

In "The Moral Background," Santayana undertakes to survey the philosophical influences that lay behind the genteel tradition and to characterize its intellectual qualities in its heyday in the nineteenth century. This is ground that he has partly covered before and will return to again, but here his focus is steadiest and most intense. Nowhere are we made more keenly aware of how misguided and in error he considered the American intellectual tradition to be, and how fitting he thought it was that its modern heirs should abandon it without bothering to refute it.

This essay is reprinted from *Character and Opinion in the United States* (New York: Charles Scribner's Sons, 1920).

About the middle of the nineteenth century, in the quiet sunshine of provincial prosperity, New England had an Indian summer of the mind; and an agreeable reflective literature showed how brilliant that russet and yellow season could be. There were poets, historians, orators, preachers, most of whom had studied foreign literatures and had travelled; they demurely kept up with the times; they were universal humanists. But it was all a harvest of leaves; these worthies had an expurgated and barren conception of life; theirs was the purity of sweet old age. Sometimes they made attempts to rejuvenate their minds by broaching native subjects; they wished to prove how much matter for poetry the new world supplied, and they wrote "Rip van Winkle," "Hiawatha," or "Evangeline"; but the inspiration did not seem much more American than that of Swift or Ossian or Chateaubriand. These cultivated writers lacked native roots and fresh sap because the American intellect itself lacked them. Their culture was half a pious survival, half an intentional acquirement; it was not the inevitable flowering of a fresh experience. Later there have been admirable analytic novelists who have depicted American life as it is, but rather bitterly, rather sadly; as if the joy and the illusion of it did not inspire them, but only an abstract interest in their own art. If any one, like Walt Whitman, penetrated to the feelings and images which the

American scene was able to breed out of itself, and filled them with a frank and broad afflatus of his own, there is no doubt that he misrepresented the conscious minds of cultivated Americans; in them the head as yet did not belong to the trunk.

Nevertheless, *belles-lettres* in the United States—which after all stretch beyond New England—have always had two points of contact with the great national experiment. One point of contact has been oratory, with that sort of poetry, patriotic, religious, or moral, which has the function of oratory. Eloquence is a republican art, as conversation is an aristocratic one. By eloquence at public meetings and dinners, in the pulpit or in the press, the impulses of the community could be brought to expression; consecrated maxims could be reapplied; the whole latent manliness and shrewdness of the nation could be mobilised. In the form of oratory reflection, rising out of the problems of action, could be turned to guide or to sanction action, and sometimes could attain, in so doing, a notable elevation of thought. Although Americans, and many other people, usually say that thought is for the sake of action, it has evidently been in these high moments, when action became incandescent in thought, that they have been most truly alive, intensively most active, and although *doing* nothing, have found at last that their existence was worth while. Reflection is itself a turn, and the top turn, given to life. Here is the second point at which literature in America has fused with the activities of the nation: it has paused to enjoy them. Every animal has his festive and ceremonious moments, when he poses or plumes himself or thinks; sometimes he even sings and flies aloft in a sort of ecstasy. Somewhat in the same way, when reflection in man becomes dominant, it may become passionate; it may create religion or philosophy—adventures often more thrilling than the humdrum experience they are supposed to interrupt.

This pure flame of mind is nothing new, superadded, or alien in America. It is notorious how metaphysical was the passion that drove the Puritans to those shores; they went there in the hope of living more perfectly in the spirit. And their pilgrim's progress was not finished when they had founded their churches in the wilderness; an endless migration of the mind was still before them, a flight from those new idols and servitudes which prosperity involves, and the eternal lure of spiritual freedom and truth. The moral world always contains undiscovered or thinly peopled continents open to those who are more attached to what might or should be than to what already is. Americans are eminently prophets; they apply morals to public affairs; they are impatient and enthusiastic. Their judgments have highly speculative implications, which they often make explicit; they are men with principles, and fond of stating them. Moreover, they have an intense self-reliance; to exercise private judgment is not only a habit with them but a conscious duty. Not seldom personal conversions and mystical experiences throw their ingrained faith into novel forms, which may be very bold and radical. They are traditionally exercised about religion, and adrift on the subject more than any other people on earth; and if religion is a dreaming philosophy, and philosophy a waking religion, a people so wide awake and so religious as the old Yankees ought certainly to have been rich in philosophers.

In fact, philosophy in the good old sense of curiosity about the nature of things, with readiness to make the best of them, has not been absent from the practice of Americans or from their humourous moods; their humour and shrewdness are sly comments on the shortcomings of some polite convention that everybody accepts tacitly, yet feels to be insecure and contrary to the principles on which life is actually carried on. Nevertheless, with the shyness which simple competence often shows in the presence of conventional shams, these wits have not taken their native wisdom very seriously. They have not had the leisure nor the intellectual scope to think out and defend the implications of their homely perceptions. Their fresh insight has been whispered in parentheses and asides; it has been humbly banished, in alarm, from their solemn moments. What people have respected have been rather scraps of official philosophy, or entire systems, which they have inherited or imported, as they have respected operas and art museums. To be on speaking terms with these fine things was a part of social respectability, like having family silver. High thoughts must be at hand, like those candlesticks, probably candleless, sometimes displayed as a seemly ornament in a room blazing with electric light. Even in William James, spontaneous and stimulating as he was, a certain underlying discomfort was discernible; he had come out into the open, into what should have been the sunshine, but the vast shadow of the temple still stood between him and the sun. He was worried about what *ought* to be believed and the awful deprivations of disbelieving. What he called the cynical view of anything had first to be brushed aside, without stopping to consider whether it was not the true one; and he was bent on finding new and empirical reasons for clinging to free-will, departed spirits, and tutelary gods. Nobody, except perhaps in this last decade, has tried to bridge the chasm between what he believes in daily life and the "problems" of philosophy. Nature and science have not been ignored, and "practice" in some schools has been constantly referred to; but instead of supplying philosophy with its data they have only constituted its difficulties; its function has been not to build on known facts but to explain them away. Hence a curious alternation and irrelevance, as between weekdays and Sabbaths, between American ways and American opinions.

That philosophy should be attached to tradition would be a great advantage, conducive to mutual understanding, to maturity, and to progress, if the tradition lay in the highway of truth. To deviate from it in that case would be to betray the fact that, while one might have a lively mind, one was not master of the subject. Unfortunately, in the nineteenth century, in America as elsewhere, the ruling tradition was not only erratic and far from the highway of truth, but the noonday of this tradition was over, and its classic forms were outgrown. A philosophy may have a high value, other than its truth to things, in its truth to method and to the genius of its author; it may be a feat of synthesis and imagination, like a great poem, expressing one of the eternal possibilities of being, although one which the creator happened to reject when he made this world. It is possible to be a master in false philosophy—easier, in fact, than to be a master in the truth, because a false philosophy can be made as simple and consistent as one pleases. Such had been the masters of the tradition prevalent in New England—Calvin, Hume, Fichte, not to mention others more relished because less pure; but one of the disadvantages of such perfection in error is that the illusion is harder to transmit to another age and country. If Jonathan Edwards, for instance, was a Calvinist of pristine force and perhaps the greatest *master* in false philosophy that America has yet produced, he paid the price by being abandoned, even in his lifetime, by his own sect, and seeing the world turn a deaf ear to his logic without so much as attempting to refute it. One of the peculiarities of recent speculation, especially in America, is that ideas are abandoned in virtue of a mere change of feeling, without any new evidence or new arguments. We do not nowadays refute our predecessors, we pleasantly bid them good-bye. Even if all our principles are unwittingly traditional we do not like to bow openly to authority. Hence masters like Calvin, Hume, or Fichte rose before their American admirers like formidable ghosts, foreign and unseizable. People refused to be encumbered with any system, even one of their own; they were content to imbibe more or less of the spirit of a philosophy and to let it play on such facts as happened to attract their attention. The originality even of Emerson and of William James was of this incidental character; they found new approaches to old beliefs or new expedients in old dilemmas. They were not in a scholastic sense pupils of anybody or masters in anything. They hated the scholastic way of saying what they meant, if they had heard of it; they insisted on a personal freshness of style, refusing to make their thought more precise than it happened to be spontaneously; and they lisped their logic, when the logic came.

We must remember that ever since the days of Socrates, and especially after the establishment of Christianity, the dice of thought have been loaded. Certain pledges have preceded inquiry and divided the possible conclusions before hand into the acceptable and the inacceptable, the edifying and the shocking, the noble and the base. Wonder has no longer been the root of philosophy, but sometimes impatience at having been cheated and sometimes fear of being undeceived. The marvel of existence, in which the luminous and the opaque are so romantically mingled, no longer lay like a sea open to intellectual adventure, tempting the mind to conceive some bold and curious system of the universe on the analogy of what had been so far discovered. Instead, people were confronted with an orthodoxy —though not always the same orthodoxy—whispering mysteries and brandishing anathemas. Their wits were absorbed in solving traditional problems, many of them artificial and such as the ruling orthodoxy had created by its gratuitous assumptions. Difficulties were therefore found in some perfectly obvious truths; and obvious fables, if they were hallowed by association, were seriously weighed in the balance against one another or against the facts; and many an actual thing was proved to be impossible, or was hidden under a false description. In conservative schools the student learned and tried to fathom the received solutions; in liberal schools he was perhaps invited to seek solutions of his own, but still to the old questions. Freedom, when nominally allowed, was a provisional freedom; if your wanderings did not somehow bring you back to orthodoxy you were a misguided being, no matter how disparate from the orthodox might be the field from which you fetched your little harvest; and if you could not be answered you were called superficial. Most spirits are cowed by such disparagement; but even those who snap their fingers at it do not escape; they can hardly help feeling that in calling a spade a spade they are petulant and naughty; or if their inspiration is too genuine for that, they still unwittingly shape their opinions in contrast to those that claim authority, and therefore on the same false lines—a terrible tax to pay to the errors of others; and it is only here and there that a very great and solitary mind, like that of Spinoza, can endure obloquy without bitterness or can pass through perverse controversies without contagion. | *important*

Under such circumstances it is obvious that speculation can be frank and happy only where orthodoxy has receded, abandoning a larger and larger field to unprejudiced inquiry; or else (as has happened among liberal Protestants) where the very heart of orthodoxy has melted, has absorbed the most alien substances, and is ready to bloom into anything that anybody finds attractive. This is the secret of that extraordinary vogue which the transcendental philosophy has had for nearly a century in Great Britain and America; it is a method which enables a man to renovate all his beliefs, scientific and religious, from the inside, giving them a new status and interpretation as phases of his own experience or imagination; so that he does not seem to himself to reject anything, and yet is bound to nothing, except to his creative self. Many too who have no inclination to practice this transcendental method—a personal, arduous, and futile art, which requires to be renewed at every moment—have been impressed with the results or the maxims of this or that transcendental philosopher, such as that every opinion leads on to another that reinterprets it, or every evil to some higher good that contains it; and they have managed to identify these views with what still seemed to them vital in religion. |

In spite of this profound mutation at the core, and much paring at the edges, traditional belief in New England retained its continuity and its priestly unction; and religious teachers and philosophers could slip away from Calvinism and even from Christianity without any loss of elevation or austerity. They found it so pleasant and easy to elude the past that they really had no quarrel with it. The world, they felt, was a safe place, watched over by a kindly God, who exacted nothing but cheerfulness and good-will from his children; and the American flag was a sort of rainbow in the sky, promising that all storms were over. Or if storms came, such as the Civil War, they would not be harder to weather than was necessary to test the national spirit and raise it to a new efficiency. The subtler dangers which we may now see threatening America had not yet come in sight—material restlessness was not yet ominous, the pressure of business enterprises was not yet out of scale with the old life or out of key with the old moral harmonies. A new type of American had not appeared—the untrained, pushing, cosmopolitan orphan, cock-sure in manner but not too sure in his morality, to whom the old Yankee, with his sour integrity, is almost a foreigner. Was not "increase," in the Bible, a synonym for benefit? Was not "abundance" the same, or almost the same, as happiness?

Meantime the churches, a little ashamed of their past, began to court the good opinion of so excellent a world. Although called evangelical, they were far, very far, from prophesying its end, or offering a refuge from it, or preaching contempt for it; they existed only to serve it, and their highest divine credential was that the world needed them. Irreligion, dissoluteness, and pessimism—supposed naturally to go together—could never prosper; they were incompatible with efficiency. That was the supreme test. "Be Christians," I once heard a president of Yale College cry to his assembled pupils, "be Christians and you will be successful." Religion was indispensable and sacred, when not carried too far; but theology might well be unnecessary. Why distract this world with talk of another? Enough for the day was the good thereof. Religion should be disentangled as much as possible from history and authority and metaphysics, and made to rest honestly on one's fine feelings, on one's indomitable optimism and trust in life. Revelation was nothing miraculous, given once for all in some remote age and foreign country; it must come to us directly, and with greater authority now than ever before. If evolution was to be taken seriously and to include moral growth, the great men of the past could only be stepping-stones to our own dignity. To grow was to contain and sum up all the good that had gone before, adding an appropriate increment. Undoubtedly some early figures were beautiful, and allowances had to be made for local influences in Palestine, a place so much more primitive and backward than Massachusetts. Jesus was a prophet more winsome and nearer to ourselves than his predecessors; but how could any one deny that the twenty centuries of progress since his time must have raised a loftier pedestal for Emerson or Channing or Phillips Brooks? It might somehow not be in good taste to put this feeling into clear words; one and perhaps two of these men would have deprecated it; nevertheless it beamed with refulgent self-satisfaction in the lives and maxims of most of their followers.

All this liberalism, however, never touched the centre of traditional orthodoxy, and those who, for all their modernness, felt that they inherited the faith of their fathers and were true to it were fundamentally right. There was still an orthodoxy among American highbrows at the end of the nineteenth century, dissent from which was felt to be

scandalous; it consisted in holding that the universe exists
and is governed for the sake of man or of the human spirit.
This persuasion, arrogant as it might seem, is at bottom an
expression of impotence rather than of pride. The soul is
originally vegetative; it feels the weal and woe of what
occurs within the body. With locomotion and the instinct
to hunt and to flee, animals begin to notice external things
also; but the chief point noticed about them is whether
they are good or bad; friendly or hostile, far or near. The
station of the animal and his interests thus become the
measure of all things for him, in so far as he knows them;
and this aspect of them is, by a primitive fatality, the heart
of them to him. It is only reason that can discount these
childish perspectives, neutralise the bias of each by collat-
ing it with the others, and masterfully conceive the field in
which their common objects are deployed, discovering also
the principle of foreshortening or projection which produces each perspective in turn. But reason is a later comer
into this world, and weak; against its suasion stands the
mighty resistance of habit and of moral presumption. It is
in their interest, and to rehabilitate the warm vegetative
autonomy of the primitive soul, that orthodox religion and
philosophy labour in the western world—for the mind of
India cannot be charged with this folly. Although inwardly
these systems have not now a good conscience and do not
feel very secure (for they are retrograde and sin against
the light), yet outwardly they are solemn and venerable;
and they have incorporated a great deal of moral wisdom
with their egotism or humanism—more than the Indians
with their respect for the infinite. In deifying human interests they have naturally studied and expressed them justly,
whereas those who perceive the relativity of human goods
are tempted to scorn them—which is itself unreasonable—

and to sacrifice them all to the single passion of worship or of despair. Hardly anybody, except possibly the Greeks at their best, has realised the sweetness and glory of being a rational animal.

The Jews, as we know, had come to think that it was the creator of the world, the God of the universe, who had taken them for his chosen people. Christians in turn had asserted that it was God in person who, having become a man, had founded their church. According to this Hebraic tradition, the dignity of man did not lie in being a mind (which he undoubtedly is) but in being a creature materially highly favoured, with a longer life and a brighter destiny than other creatures in the world. It is remarkable how deep, in the Hebraic religions, is this interest in material existence; so deep that we are surprised when we discover that, according to the insight of other races, this interest is the essence of irreligion. Some detachment from existence and from hopes of material splendour has indeed filtered into Christianity through Platonism. Socrates and his disciples admired this world, but they did not particularly covet it, or wish to live long in it, or expect to improve it; what they cared for was an idea or a good which they found expressed in it, something outside it and timeless, in which the contemplative intellect might be literally absorbed. This philosophy was no less humanistic than that of the Jews, though in a less material fashion: if it did not read the universe in terms of thrift, it read it in terms of art. The pursuit of a good, such as is presumably aimed at in human action, was supposed to inspire every movement in nature; and this good, for the sake of which the very heavens revolved, was akin to the intellectual happiness of a Greek sage. Nature was a philosopher in pursuit of an idea. Natural science then took a moralising turn which it has not yet quite outgrown. Socrates required of astronomy, if it was to be true science, that it should show why *it was best* that the sun and moon should be as they are; and Plato, refining on this, assures us that the eyes are placed in the front of the head, rather than at the back, because the front is the nobler quarter, and that the intestines are long in order that we may have leisure between meals to study philosophy. Curiously enough, the very enemies of final causes sometimes catch this infection and attach absolute values to facts in an opposite sense and in an inhuman interest; and you often hear in America that whatever is is right. These naturalists, while they rebuke the moralists for thinking that nature is ruled magically for our good, think her adorable for being ruled, in scorn of us, only by her own laws; and thus we oscillate between egotism and idolatry.

The Reformation did not reform this belief in the cosmic supremacy of man, or the humanity of God; on the contrary, it took it (like so much else) in terrible German earnest, not suffering it any longer to be accepted somewhat lightly as a classical figure of speech or a mystery resting on revelation. The human race, the chosen people, the Christian elect were like tabernacle within tabernacle for the spirit; but in the holy of holies was the spirit itself, one's own spirit and experience, which was the centre of everything. Protestant philosophy, exploring the domain of science and history with confidence, and sure of finding the spirit walking there, was too conscientious to misrepresent what it found. As the terrible facts could not be altered they had to be undermined. By turning psychology into metaphysics this could be accomplished, and we could reach the remarkable conclusion that the human spirit was not so much the purpose of the universe as its seat, and the only universe there was.

This conclusion, which sums up idealism on its critical or scientific side, would not of itself give much comfort to religious minds, that usually crave massive support rather than sublime independence; it leads to the heroic egotism of Fichte or Nietzsche rather than to any green pastures beside any still waters. But the critical element in idealism can be used to destroy belief in the natural world; and by so doing it can open the way to another sort of idealism, not at all critical, which might be called the higher superstition. This views the world as an oracle or charade, concealing a dramatic unity, or formula, or maxim, which all experience exists to illustrate. The habit of regarding existence as a riddle, with a surprising solution which we think we have found, should be the source of rather mixed emotions; the facts remain as they were, and rival solutions may at any time suggest themselves; and the one we have hit on may not, after all, be particularly comforting. The Christian may find himself turned by it into a heathen, the humanist into a pantheist, and the hope with which we instinctively faced life may be chastened into mere conformity. Nevertheless, however chilling and inhuman our higher superstition may prove, it will make us feel that we are masters of a mystical secret, that we have a faith to defend, and that, like all philosophers, we have taken a ticket in a lottery in which if we hit on the truth, even if it seems a blank, we shall have drawn the first prize.

Orthodoxy in New England, even so transformed and attenuated, did not of course hold the field alone. There are materialists by instinct in every age and country; there are always private gentlemen whom the clergy and the professors cannot deceive. Here and there a medical or scientific man, or a man of letters, will draw from his special pursuits some hint of the nature of things at large; or a political radical will nurse undying wrath against all opinions not tartly hostile to church and state. But these clever people are not organised, they are not always given to writing, nor speculative enough to make a system out of their convictions. The enthusiasts and the pedagogues naturally flock to the other camp. The very competence which scientific people and connoisseurs have in their special fields disinclines them to generalise, or renders their generalisations one-sided; so that their speculations are extraordinarily weak and stammering. Both by what they represent and by what they ignore they are isolated and deprived of influence, since only those who are at home in a subject can feel the force of analogies drawn from that field, whereas any one can be swayed by sentimental and moral appeals, by rhetoric and unction. Furthermore, in America the materialistic school is without that support from popular passions which it draws in many European countries from its association with anticlericalism or with revolutionary politics; and it also lacks the maturity, self-confidence, and refinement proper in older societies to the great body of Epicurean and disenchanted opinion, where for centuries wits, critics, minor philosophers, and men of the world have chuckled together over their Horace, their Voltaire, and their Gibbon. The horror which the theologians have of infidelity passes therefore into the average American mind unmitigated by the suspicion that anything pleasant could lie in that quarter, much less the open way to nature and truth and a secure happiness.

There is another handicap, of a more technical sort, under

which naturalistic philosophy labours in America, as it does in England; it has been crossed by scepticism about the validity of perception and has become almost identical with psychology. Of course, for any one who thinks naturalistically (as the British empiricists did in the beginning, like every unsophisticated mortal) psychology is the description of a very superficial and incidental complication in the animal kingdom: it treats of the curious sensibility and volatile thoughts awakened in the mind by the growth and fortunes of the body. In noting these thoughts and feelings, we can observe how far they constitute true knowledge of the world in which they arise, how far they ignore it, and how far they play with it, by virtue of the poetry and the syntax of discourse which they add out of their own exuberance; for fancy is a very fertile treacherous thing, as every one finds when he dreams. But dreams run over into waking life, and sometimes seem to permeate and to underlie it; and it was just this suspicion that he might be dreaming awake, that discourse and tradition might be making a fool of him, that prompted the hard-headed Briton, even before the Reformation, to appeal from conventional beliefs to "experience." He was anxious to clear away those sophistries and impostures of which he was particularly apprehensive, in view of the somewhat foreign character of his culture and religion. Experience, he thought, would bear unimpeachable witness to the nature of things; for by experience he understood knowledge produced by direct contact with the object. Taken in this sense, experience is a method of discovery, an exercise of intelligence; it is the same observation of things, strict, cumulative, and analytic, which produces the natural sciences. It rests on naturalistic assumptions (since we know when and where we find our data) and could not fail to end in materialism. What prevented British empiricism from coming to this obvious conclusion was a peculiarity of the national temperament. The Englishman is not only distrustful of too much reasoning and too much theory (and science and materialsm involve a good deal of both), but he is also fond of musing and of withdrawing into his inner man. Accordingly his empiricism took an introspective form; like Hamlet he stopped at the *how*; he began to think about thinking. His first care was now to arrest experience as he underwent it; though its presence could not be denied, it came in such a questionable shape that it could not be taken at its word. This mere presence of experience, this ghostly apparition to the inner man, was all that empirical philosophy could now profess to discover. Far from being an exercise of intelligence, it retracted all understanding, all interpretation, all instinctive faith; far from furnishing a sure record of the truths of nature, it furnished a set of pathological facts, the passive subject-matter of psychology. These now seemed the only facts admissible, and psychology, for the philosophers, became the only science. Experience could discover nothing, but all discoveries had to be retracted, so that they should revert to the fact of experience and terminate there. Evidently when the naturalistic background and meaning of experience have dropped out in this way, empiricism is a form of idealism, since whatever objects we can come upon will all be *a priori* and *a fortiori* and *sensu eminentiori* ideal in the mind. The irony of logic actually made English empiricism, understood in this psychological way, the starting-point for transcendentalism and for German philosophy.

Between these two senses of the word experience, meaning sometimes contact with things and at other times absolute feeling, the empirical school in England and America has been helplessly torn, without ever showing the courage or the self-knowledge to choose between them. I think we may say that on the whole their view has been this: that feelings or ideas were absolute atoms of existence, without any ground or source, so that the elements of their universe were all mental; but they conceived these psychical elements to be deployed in a physical time and even (since there were many simultaneous series of them) in some sort of space. These philosophers were accordingly idealists about substance but naturalists about the order and relations of existences; and experience on their lips meant feeling when they were thinking of particulars, but when they were thinking broadly, in matters of history or science, experience meant the universal nebula or cataract which these feelings composed—itself no object of experience, but one believed in and very imperfectly presented in imagination. These men believed in nature, and were materialists at heart and to all practical purposes; but they were shy intellectually, and seemed to think they ran less risk of error in holding a thing covertly than in openly professing it.

If any one, like Herbert Spencer, kept psychology in its place and in that respect remained a pure naturalist, he often forfeited this advantage by enveloping the positive information he derived from the sciences in a whirlwind of generalisations. The higher superstition, the notion that nature dances to the tune of some comprehensive formula or some magic rhyme, thus reappeared among those who claimed to speak for natural science. In their romantic sympathy with nature they attributed to her an excessive sympathy with themselves; they overlooked her infinite complications and continual irony, and candidly believed they could measure her with their thumb-rules. Why should philosophers drag a toy-net of words, fit to catch butterflies, through the sea of being, and expect to land all the fish in it? Why not take note simply of what the particular sciences can as yet tell us of the world? Certainly, when put together, they already yield a very wonderful, very true, and very sufficient picture of it. Are we impatient of knowing everything? But even if science was much enlarged it would have limits, both in penetration and in extent; and there would always remain, I will not say an infinity of unsolved problems (because "problems" are created by our impatience or our contradictions), but an infinity of undiscovered facts. Nature is like a beautiful woman that may be as delightfully and as truly known at a certain distance as upon a closer view; as to knowing her through and through, that is nonsense in both cases, and might not reward our pains. The love of all-inclusiveness is as dangerous in philosophy as in art. The savour of nature can be enjoyed by us only through our own senses and insight, and an outline map of the entire universe, even if it was not fabulously concocted, would not tell us much that was worth knowing about the outlying parts of it. Without suggesting for a moment that the proper study of mankind is man only—for it may be landscape or mathematics—we may safely say that their proper study is what lies within their range and is interesting to them. For this reason the moralists who consider principally human life and paint nature only as a background to their figures are apt to be better philosophers than the speculative naturalists. In human life we are at home, and our views on it, if one-sided, are for that very reason expressive of our character and fortunes. An unfortunate peculiarity of naturalistic philosophers is that usually they have but cursory and wretched notions of the inner life of the mind; they are dead to patriotism and to religion, they hate poetry and fancy and passion and even philosophy itself; and therefore (especially if their science too, as often happens, is borrowed and vague) we need not wonder if the academic and cultivated world despises them, and harks back to the mythology of Plato or Aristotle or Hegel, who at least were conversant with the spirit of man.

Philosophers are very severe towards other philosophers because they expect too much. Even under the most favourable circumstances no mortal can be asked to seize the truth in its wholeness or at its centre. As the senses open to us only partial perspectives, taken from one point of view, and report the facts in symbols which, far from being adequate to the full nature of what surrounds us, resemble the coloured signals of danger or of free way which a railway engine-driver peers at in the night, so our speculation, which is a sort of panoramic sense, approaches things peripherally and expresses them humanly. But how doubly dyed in this subjectivity must our thought be when an orthodoxy dominant for ages has twisted the universe into the service of moral interests, and when even the heretics are entangled in a scepticism so partial and arbitrary that it substitutes psychology, the most derivative and dubious of sciences, for the direct intelligent reading of experience! But this strain of subjectivity is not in all respects an evil; it is a warm purple dye. When a way of thinking is deeply rooted in the soil, and embodies the instincts or even the characteristic errors of a people, it has a value quite independent of its truth; it constitutes a phase of human life and can powerfully affect the intellectual drama in which it figures. It is a value of this sort that attaches to modern philosophy in general, and very particularly to the American thinkers I am about to discuss. There would be a sort of irrelevance and unfairness in measuring them by the standards of pure science or even of a classic sagacity, and reproaching them for not having reached perfect consistency or fundamental clearness. Men of intense feeling— and others will hardly count—are not mirrors but lights. If pure truth happened to be what they passionately desired, they would seek it single-mindedly, and in matters within their competence they would probably find it; but the desire for pure truth, like any other, must wait to be satisfied until its organ is ripe and the conditions are favourable. The nineteenth century was not a time and America was not a place where such an achievement could be expected. There the wisest felt themselves to be, as they were, questioners and apostles rather than serene philosophers. We should not pay them the doubtful compliment of attributing to them merits alien to their tradition and scope, as if the nobleness they actually possessed—their conscience, vigour, timeliness, and influence—were not enough.

Philosophical Opinion in America

This essay was delivered as an address before the British Academy in January 1918 as the "Third Annual Philosophical Lecture" under the auspices of the Henriette Hertz Trust and subsequently included, with few changes, in *Character and Opinion in the United States.* There it follows chapters on William James and Josiah Royce and is called "Later Speculations," which fixes its focus more precisely than the original title. The subject is not the genteel tradition itself so much as its philosophic successors, particularly the school Santayana calls the "new realists," but the discussion entails a differentiation between the former and the latter that adds significantly to his total characterization of the genteel tradition. Here the theme of the two mentalities is taken up again, and the influence of the old upon the new is assessed in such a way that, although the bulk of the essay is given over to a consideration of the later, nongenteel speculation, the genteel tradition plays an important role. His stated intention, to inquire how migration to the new world has affected philosophical ideas, works itself out almost inevitably with Santayana finding the expression of "a certain despairing democracy in the field of opinion."

"Philosophical Opinion in America" is reprinted from the *British Academy: Proceedings*, VIII (1917-1918). It was reprinted, slightly revised, as Chapter V, "Later Speculations," in *Character and Opinion in the United States* (New York: Charles Scribner's Sons, 1920).

The honour of addressing the British Academy is not one to be declined; and in considering on what subject a not very learned person might venture to do so, it has occurred to me that I might profit by my long association with academic philosophers in America to put before you some observations on a question which is curious in itself and may become important in the future; namely, how has migration to the new world affected philosophical ideas?

At first sight we might be tempted, perhaps, to dismiss this question altogether, on the ground that no such effect is discernible. For what do we find in America in the guise of philosophy? In the background the same Protestant theology as in Europe and the same Catholic theology; on the surface, the same adoption of German idealism, the same vogue of evolution, the same psychology becoming metaphysics, and lately the same revival of a mathematical or logical realism. In no case has the first expression of these various tendencies appeared in America, and no original system that I know of has arisen there. It would seem, then, that in philosophy, as in letters generally, polite America has continued the common tradition of Christendom, in paths closely parallel to those followed in England; and that modern speculation, which is so very sensitive to changed times, is quite indifferent to distinctions of place.

Perhaps; but I say advisedly *polite* America, for without this qualification what I have been suggesting would hardly be true. Polite America carried over its household gods from Puritan England in a spirit of consecration, and it has always wished to remain in communion with whatever its conscience might value in the rest of the world. Yet it has been cut off by distance and by revolutionary prejudice against things ancient or foreign; and it has been disconcerted at the same time by the insensible shifting of the ground under its feet: it has suffered from in-breeding and anaemia. On the other hand, a crude but vital America has sprung up from the soil, undermining, feeding, and transforming the America of tradition.

This young America was originally composed of all the prodigals, truants, and adventurous spirits that the colonial families produced: it was fed continually by the younger generation, born in a spacious, half-empty world, tending to forget the old straitened morality and to replace it by another, quite jovially human. This truly native America was reinforced by the miscellany of Europe arriving later, not in the hope of founding a godly commonwealth, but only of prospering in an untrammelled one. The horde of immigrants eagerly accepts the external arrangements and social spirit of American life, but never hears of its original austere principles, or relegates them to the same willing oblivion as it does the constraints which it has just escaped —Jewish, Irish, German, Italian, or whatever they may be. We should be seriously deceived if we overlooked for a moment the curious and complex relation between these two Americas.

Let me give you one illustration. Professor Norton, the

friend of Carlyle, of Ruskin, and of Matthew Arnold, and, for the matter of that, the friend of everybody, a most urbane, learned, and exquisite spirit, was descended from the most typical of New England divines: yet he was loudly accused, in public and in private, of being un-American. On the other hand, a Frenchman of ripe judgement, who knew him perfectly, once said to me: 'Norton wouldn't like to hear it, but he is a terrible Yankee.' Both judgements were well grounded. Professor Norton's mind was deeply moralized, discriminating, and sad; and these qualities rightly seemed American to the French observer of New England, but they rightly seemed un-American to the politician from Washington.

Philosophical opinion in America is of course rooted in the genteel tradition. It is either inspired by religious faith, and designed to defend it, or else it is created somewhat artificially in the larger universities, by deliberately proposing problems which, without being very pressing to most Americans, are supposed to be necessary problems of thought. Yet if you expected academic philosophers in America, because the background of their minds seems perfunctory, to resemble academic philosophers elsewhere, you would be often mistaken. There is no prig's paradise in those regions. Many of the younger professors of philosophy are no longer the sort of persons that might as well have been clergymen or schoolmasters: they have rather the type of mind of a doctor, an engineer, or a social reformer; the wide-awake young man who can do most things better than old people, and who knows it. He is less eloquent and apostolic than the older generation of philosophers, very professional in tone and conscious of his *Fach;* not that he would deny for a moment the many-sided ignorance to which nowadays we are all reduced, but that he thinks he can get on very well without the things he ignores. His education has been more pretentious than thorough; his style is deplorable; social pressure and his own great eagerness have condemned him to over-work, committee meetings, early marriage, premature authorship, and lecturing two or three times a day under forced draught. He has no peace in himself, no window open to a calm horizon, and in his heart perhaps little taste for mere scholarship or pure speculation. Yet like the plain soldier staggering under his clumsy equipment, he is cheerful; he keeps his faith in himself and in his allotted work, puts up with being toasted only on one side, remains open-minded, whole-hearted, appreciative, helpful, confident of the future of goodness and of science. In a word, he is a cell in that teeming democratic body; he draws from its warm, contagious activities the sanctions of his own life and, less consciously, the spirit of his philosophy.

It is evident that such minds will have but a loose hold on tradition, even on the genteel tradition in American philosophy. Not that in general they oppose or dislike it; their alienation from it is more radical; they forget it. Religion was the backbone of that tradition, and towards religion, in so far as it is a private sentiment or presumption, they feel a tender respect; but in so far as religion is a political institution, seeking to coerce the mind and the conscience, one would think they had never heard of it. They feel it is as much every one's right to choose and cherish a religion as to choose and cherish a wife, without having his choice rudely commented upon in public. Hitherto America has been the land of universal goodwill, confidence in life, inexperience of poisons. Until yesterday it believed itself

immune from the hereditary plagues of mankind. It could
not credit the danger of being suffocated or infected by any
sinister principle. The more errors and passions were thrown
into the melting-pot, the more certainly would they neutralize one another and would truth come to the top. Every
system was met with a frank gaze. 'Come on' people seemed
to say to it, 'show us what you are good for. We accept no
claims; we ask for no credentials; we just give you a chance.
Plato, the Pope, and Mrs. Eddy shall have one vote each.'
After all, I am not sure that this toleration without deference is not a cruel test for systematic delusions; it lets the
daylight into the stage.

Philosophic tradition in America has merged almost completely in German idealism. In a certain sense this system
did not need to be adopted: something very like it had
grown up spontaneously in New England in the form of
transcendentalism and Unitarian theology. Even the most
emancipated and positivistic of the latest thinkers—pragmatists, new realists, pure empiricists—have been bred in
the atmosphere of German idealism; and this fact should
not be forgotten in approaching their views. The element
of this philosophy which has sunk deepest, and which is
reinforced by the influence of psychology, is the critical
attitude towards knowledge, subjectivism, withdrawal into
experience, on the assumption that experience is something
substantial. Experience was regarded by earlier empiricists
as a method for making real discoveries, a safer witness
than reasoning to what might exist in nature; but now experience is taken to be in itself the only real existence, the
ultimate object that all thought and theory must regard.
This empiricism does not look to the building up of science,
but rather to a more thorough criticism and disintegration

of conventional beliefs, those of empirical science included. It is in the intrepid prosecution of this criticism and disintegration that American philosophy has won its wings.

It may seem a strange Nemesis that a critical philosophy, which on principle reduces everything to the consciousness of it, should end by reducing consciousness itself to other things; yet the path of this boomerang is not hard to trace. The word consciousness originally meant what Descartes called thought or cogitation—the faculty which attention has of viewing together objects which may belong together neither in their logical essence nor in their natural existence. It colours events with memories and facts with emotions, and adds images to words. This synthetic and transitive function of consciousness is a positive fact about it, to be discovered by study, like any other somewhat recondite fact. You will discover it if you institute a careful comparison and contrast between the way things hang together in thought and the way they hang together in nature. To have discerned the wonderful perspectives both of imagination and of will seems to me the chief service done to philosophy by Kant and his followers. It is the positive, the non-malicious element in their speculation; and in the midst of their psychologism in logic and their egotism about nature, and history, consciousness seems to be the one province of being which they have thrown true light upon. But just because this is a positive province of being, an actual existence to be discovered and dogmatically believed in, it is not what a malicious criticism of knowledge can end with. Not the nature of consciousness, but the data of consciousness, are what the critic must fall back upon in the last resort; and Hume had been in this respect a more penetrating critic than Kant. One cannot, by inspecting consciousness, find consciousness itself as a passive datum, because consciousness is cogitation; one can only take note of the immediate objects of consciousness, in such private perspective as sense or imagination may present.

Philosophy seems to be richer in theories than in words to express them in; and much confusion results from the necessity of using old terms in new meanings. In this way, when consciousness is disregarded, in the proper sense of cogitation, the name of consciousness can be transferred to the stream of objects immediately present to consciousness; so that consciousness comes to signify the evolving field of appearances unrolled before any person.

This equivocation is favoured by the allied ambiguity of an even commoner term, idea. It is plausible to say that consciousness is a stream of ideas, because an idea may mean an opinion, a cogitation, a view taken of some object. And it is also plausible to say that ideas are objects of consciousness, because an idea may mean an image, a passive datum. Passive data may be of any sort you like—things, qualities, relations, propositions—but they are never cogitations; and to call *them* consciousness or components of consciousness is false and inexcusable. The ideas that may be so called are not these passive objects, but active thoughts. Indeed, when the psychological critic has made this false step, he is not able to halt: his method will carry him presently from this position to one even more paradoxical.

Is memory knowledge of a past that is itself absent and dead, or is it a present experience? A complete philosophy would doubtless reply that it is both; but psychological criticism can take cognizance of memory only as a mass of present images and presumptions. The experience remembered may indeed be exactly recovered and be present again; but the fact that it was present before cannot possibly be given now; it can only be suggested and believed.

It is evident, therefore, that the historical order in which data flow is not contained bodily in any one of them. This order is conceived; the hypothesis is framed instinctively and instinctively credited, but it is only an hypothesis. And it is often wrong, as is proved by all the constitutional errors of memory and legend. Belief in the order of our personal experiences is accordingly just as dogmatic, daring, and realistic as the parallel belief in a material world. The psychological critic must attribute both beliefs to a mere tendency to feign; and if he is true to his method he must discard the notion that the objects of consciousness are arranged in psychological sequences, making up separate minds. In other words he must discard the notion of consciousness, not only in the sense of thought or cogitation, but in the sense he himself had given it of a stream of ideas. Actual objects, he will not admit, not without a certain surprise, are not ideas at all: they do not lie in the mind (for there is no mind to be found) but in the medium that observably surrounds them. Things are just what they seem to be, and to say they are consciousness or compose a consciousness is absurd. The so-called appearances, according to a perfected criticism of knowledge, are nothing private or internal; they are merely those portions of external objects which from time to time impress themselves on somebody's organs of sense and are responded to by his nervous system.

Such is the doctrine of the new American realists, in whose devoted persons the logic of idealism has worked itself out and appropriately turned idealism itself into its opposite. Consciousness, they began by saying, is merely a stream of ideas; but then ideas are merely the parts of objects which happen to appear to a given person; but again a person (for all you or he can discover) is nothing but his body and those parts of other objects which appear to him; and finally to appear, in any discoverable sense, cannot be to have a ghostly sort of mental existence, but merely to be reacted upon by an animal body. Thus we come to the conclusion that objects alone exist, and that consciousness is a name for certain segments or groups of these objects.

I think we may conjecture why this startling conclusion, that consciousness does not exist, a conclusion suggested somewhat hurriedly by William James, has found a considerable echo in America, and why the system of Avenarius, which makes in the same direction, has been studied there sympathetically. To deny consciousness is to deny a prerequisite to the obvious, and to leave the obvious standing alone. That is a relief to an overtaxed and self-impeded generation; it seems a blessed simplification. It gets rid of the undemocratic notion that by being very reflective, circumspect, and subtle you might discover something that most people do not see. They can go on more merrily with their work if they believe that by being so subtle, circumspect, and reflective you would only discover a mare's nest. The elimination of consciousness not only restores the obvious, but proves all parts of the obvious to be equally real. Not only colours, beauties, and passions, but all things formerly suspected of being creatures of thought, such as laws, relations, and abstract qualities, now become components of the existing object, since there is no longer any mental vehicle by which they might have been created and interposed. The young American is thus reassured: his joy in living and learning is no longer chilled by the contempt which idealism used to cast on nature for being imaginary and on science for being intellectual. All fictions and all abstractions are now declared to be parcels of the objective world; it will suffice to live on, to live forward, in order to see everything as it really is.

If we look now at these matters from a slightly different angle, we shall find psychological criticism transforming the notion of truth much as it has transformed the notion of consciousness. In the first place, there is a similar ambiguity in the term. The truth properly means the sum of all true propositions, what omniscience would assert, the whole ideal system of qualities and relations which the world has exemplified or will exemplify. The truth is all things seen under the form of eternity. In this sense, a psychological criticism cannot be pertinent to the truth at all, the truth not being anything psychological or human. It is an ideal realm of being properly enough not discussed by psychologists; yet so far as I know it is denied by nobody, not even by Protagoras or the pragmatists. If Protagoras said that whatever appears to any man at any moment is true, he doubtless meant true on that subject, true of that appearance: because for a sensualist objects do not extend beyond what he sees of them, so that each of his perceptions defines its whole object and is infallible. But in that case the truth about the universe is evidently that it is composed of these various sensations, each carrying an opinion impossible for it to abandon or to revise, since to revise the opinion would simply be to bring a fresh object into view. The truth would further be that these sensations and opinions stand to one another in certain definite relations of diversity, succession, duration, *et cætera,* whether any of them happens to assert these relations or not. In the same way, I cannot find that our contemporary pragmatists, in giving their account of what truth is (in a different and quite abstract sense of the word truth), have ever doubted, or so much as noticed, what in all their thinking they evidently assume to be the actual and concrete truth: namely, that there are many states of mind, many labouring opinions more or less useful and good, which actually lead to others, more or less expected and satisfactory. Surely every pragmatist, like every thinking man, always assumes the reality of an actual truth, comprehensive and largely undiscovered, of which he claims to be reporting a portion. What he rather confusingly calls truth, and wishes to reduce to a pragmatic function, is not this underlying truth, the sum of all true propositions, but merely the abstract quality which all true propositions must have in common, to be called true. By truth he means only correctness. The possibility of correctness in an idea is a great puzzle to him, on account of his idealism, which identifies ideas with their objects; and he asks himself how an idea can ever come to be correct or incorrect, as if it referred to something beyond itself.

The fact is, of course, that an idea can be correct or incorrect only if by the word idea we mean not a datum but an opinion; and the abstract relation of correctness, by virtue of which any opinion is true, is easily stated. An opinion is true if what it is talking about is constituted as the opinion asserts it to be constituted. To test this correctness may be difficult or even impossible in particular cases: in the end we may be reduced to believing on instinct that our fundamental opinions are true; for instance, that we are living through time, and that the past and future are not, as a consistent idealism would assert, mere notions in the present. But what renders such instinctive opinions true, if they are true, is the fact affirmed being as it is affirmed to be. It is not a question of similarity or derivation between a passive datum and a hidden object; it is a question of identity between the fact asserted and the fact existing. If an opinion could not freely leap to its object, no matter how distant or hypothetical, and assert something of that chosen object, an opinion could not be so much as wrong; for it would not be an opinion about anything.

Psychologists, however, are not concerned with what an opinion asserts logically, but only with what it is existentially; they are asking what existential relations surround an idea when it is called true which are absent when it is called false. Their problem is frankly insoluble; for it requires us to discover what makes up the indicative force of an idea which by hypothesis is a passive datum; as if a grammarian should inquire how a noun in the accusative case could be a verb in the indicative mood.

It was not idly that William James dedicated his book on Pragmatism to the memory of John Stuart Mill. The principle of psychological empiricism is to look for the elements employed in thinking and to conclude that thought is nothing but those elements arranged in a certain order. It is true that since the days of Mill analysis has somewhat extended the inventory of these elements, so as to include among simples, besides the data of the five senses, such things as feelings of relation, sensations of movement, vague ill-focused images, and perhaps even telepathic and instinctive intuitions. But some series or group of these immediate data, kept in their crude immediacy, must according to this method furnish the whole answer to our question: the supposed power of an idea to have an object beyond itself, or to be true of any other fact, must be merely a name for a certain position which the given element occupies in relation to other elements in the routine of experience. Knowledge and truth must be forms of contiguity and succession.

We must not be surprised, under these circumstances, if the problem is shifted, and another somewhat akin to it takes its place, with which the chosen method can really cope. This subterfuge is not voluntary; it is an instinctive effect of fidelity to a point of view which has its special validity, though naturally not applicable in every sphere. We do not observe that politicians abandon their party when it happens to have brought trouble upon the country; their destiny as politicians is precisely to make effective all the consequences, good or evil, which their party policy may involve. So it would be too much to expect a school of philosophers to abandon their method because there are problems it cannot solve; their business is rather to apply their method to everything to which it can possibly be applied; and when they have reached that limit, the very most we can ask, if they are superhumanly modest and wise, is that they should make way gracefully for another school of philosophers.

Now there is a problem, not impossible to confuse with the problem of correctness in ideas, with which psychological criticism can really deal: it is the question of the relation between a sign and the thing signified. Of this relation a genuinely empirical account can be given: both terms are objects of experience, present or eventual, and the passage between them is made in time by an experienced transition. Nor need the signs which lead to a particular object be always the same, or of one sort: an object may be designated and foretold unequivocally by a verbal description, without any direct image, or by images now of one sense and now of another, or by some external relation, such as its place, or by its proper name, if it possesses one; and these designations all convey knowledge of it and may be true signs, if in yielding to their suggestion we are brought eventually to the object meant.

Here, if I am not mistaken, is the genuine application of what the pragmatists call their theory of truth. It concerns merely what links a sign to the thing signified, and renders it a practical substitute for the same. But this empirical analysis of signification has been entangled with more or less hazardous views about truth, such as that an idea is true so long as it is believed to be true, or that it is true if it is good and useful, or that it is not true until it is verified. This last suggestion shows what strange reversals a wayward personal philosophy may be subject to. Empiricism used to mean reliance on the past; now apparently all empirical truth regards only the future, since truth is said to arise by the verification of some presumption. Presumptions about the past can evidently never be verified; at best they may be corroborated by fresh presumptions about the past, equally dependent for their truth on a verification which in the nature of the case is impossible. At this point the truly courageous empiricist will perhaps say that the real past only means the ideas of the past which we shall form in the future. Consistency is a jewel; and, as in the case of other jewels, we may marvel at the price that some people will pay for it. In any case, we are led to this curious result: that radical empiricism ought to deny that any idea of the past can be true at all.

Such dissolving views, really somewhat like those attributed to Protagoras, do not rest on sober psychological analysis: they express rather a certain impatience and a certain despairing democracy in the field of opinion. Great are the joys of haste and of radicalism, and young philosophers must not be deprived of them. We may the more justly pass over these small scandals of pragmatism in that William James and his American disciples have hardly cared to defend them but have turned decidedly in the direction of a universal objectivism.

The spirit of these radical views is not at all negative: it is hopeful, revolutionary, inspired entirely by love of certitude and clearness. It is very sympathetic to science, in so far as science is a personal pursuit and a personal experience, rather than a body of doctrine with moral implications. It is very close to nature, as the lover of nature understands the word. If it denies the existence of the cognitive energy and the colouring medium of mind, it does so only in a formal sense; all the colours with which that medium endows the world remain painted upon it; and all the perspectives and ideal objects of thought are woven into the texture of things. Not, I think, intelligibly or in a coherent fashion; for this new realism is still immature, and if it is ever rendered adequate it will doubtless seem much less original. My point is that in its denial of mind it has no bias against things intellectual, and if it refuses to admit ideas or even sensations, it does not blink the sensible or ideal objects which ideas and sensations reveal, but rather tries to find a new and (as it perhaps thinks) a more honourable place for them; they are not to be thought spiritual radiations from the natural world, but parts of its substance.

This may have the ring of materialism; but the temper and faith of these schools are not materialistic. Systematic materialism is one of the philosophies of old age. It is a conviction that may overtake a few shrewd and speculative cynics, who have long observed their own irrationality and that of the world, and have divined its cause: by such men materialism may be embraced without reserve, in all its rigour and pungency. But the materialism of youth is part of a simple faith in sense and in science; it is not exclusive; it admits the co-operation of any other forces—divine, magical, formal, or vital—if appearances anywhere seem to manifest them. The more we interpret the ambiguities or crudities of American writers in this sense, the less we shall misunderstand them.

It seems, then, that the atmosphere of the new world has already affected philosophy in two ways. In the first place, it has accelerated and rendered fearless the disintegration of conventional categories; a disintegration on which modern philosophy has always been at work; and which has precipitated its successive phases. In the second place, the younger cosmopolitan America has favoured the impartial assemblage and mutual confrontation of all sorts of ideas. It has produced, in intellectual matters, a sort of happy watchfulness and insecurity. Never was the human mind master of so many facts and sure of so few principles. Will this suspense and fluidity of thought crystallize into some great new system? Positive gifts of imagination and moral heroism are requisite to make a great philosopher, gifts which must come from the gods and not from circumstances. But if the genius should arise, this vast collection of suggestions and this radical analysis of presumptions which he will find in America may keep him from going astray. Nietzsche said that the earth has been a mad-house long enough. Without contradicting him we might perhaps soften the expression, and say that philosophy has been long enough an asylum for enthusiasts. It is time for it to become less solemn and more serious. We may be frightened at first to learn on what thin ice we have been skating, in speculation as in government; but we shall not be in a worse plight for knowing it, only wiser to-day and perhaps safer to-morrow.

Materialism and Idealism in America

When, in 1934, two Bryn Mawr students sent an inquiry to
Santayana concerning the following essay, he responded with a
letter that began: "What? You don't understand 'Materialism &
Idealism in American Life'? But it was written especially for a
Young Ladies College—Bedford College in Regent's Park—and
if not all in words of one syllable is surely all on one soft, sweet,
clear crystalline note. I know: because in order to determine
what I may have meant by 'moral freedom', I have had to reread the lecture."[1] His tone indicates a recognition that he had
been kinder, more forebearing, and more sympathetic toward
America in this address than he usually had been, and, in fact,
one of the most remarkable features of the piece as it relates
to the theory of the genteel tradition is the way in which it
plays down the deficiencies and dangers that Santayana had
characteristically pointed up. Delivered in the last days of the

---

[1] *The Letters of George Santayana,* ed. Daniel Cory (New York:
Charles Scribner's Sons, 1955), p. 288.

war (October 1918), "Materialism and Idealism in America" is surely colored by his warm approval of America's participation in the conflict, for his published letters sharply reveal the extent to which his general outlook had been profoundly altered by the cataclysmic outbreak of world war. When the piece was included in *Character and Opinion in the United States*, it was given the apter title referred to in the letter—apter, since its author was dealing, not with strains in America's academic philosophy, but rather with the philosophical tensions in her cultural life.

"Materialism and Idealism in America" is reprinted from *The Landmark: The Monthly Magazine of the English-Speaking Union* (London), I:1 (January 1919). It was somewhat expanded for inclusion as Chapter VI, "Materialism and Idealism in American Life," in *Character and Opinion in the United States* (New York: Charles Scribner's Sons, 1920).

The language and traditions common to England and America are like other family bonds; they draw kindred together at the greater crises of life, but they also occasion at times a little friction and fault-finding. The groundwork of the two Societies is so similar, that each nation, feeling almost at home with the other, may instinctively resent what hinders it from feeling at home altogether. Differences will tend to seem anomalies that have slipped in by mistake and through somebody's fault. Each will judge the other by his own standards, not feeling, as in the presence of complete foreigners, that he must make an effort of imagination and put himself in another man's shoes.

In matters of morals, manners and art the danger of comparisons is not merely that they may prove invidious, by ranging qualities in an order of merit which might wound somebody's vanity; the danger is rather that comparisons may distort comprehension, because good qualities all differ in kind, and free lives differ in spirit. Comparison is the expedient of those who cannot reach the heart of the things compared; and no philosophy is more external and egotistical than that which places the essence of a thing in its relation to something else. In truth, at the centre of every natural being there is something individual and incommensurable, a seed with its native impulses and aspirations, shaping themselves as best they can in their given environment. Variation is a consequence of freedom, and the slight but radical diversity of souls is what makes freedom precious.

Instead of instituting, then, any express comparisons, I would invite you, in so far as such a thing is possible for you or for me, to transport yourselves with me into the inner life of the American, to feel and enact his character dramatically, and to see how it dictates to him his judgment on himself and on all things, as they appear from his new and unobstructed station.

I speak of the American in the singular, as if there were not millions of them, north and south, east and west, of both sexes, of all ages, and of various races, professions and religions. Of course the one American I speak of is mythical; but to speak in parables is inevitable in such a subject, and it is perhaps as well to do so frankly. There is a sort of poetic ineptitude in all human discourse when it tries to deal with natural and existing things. Practical men may not notice it, but in fact human discourse is intrinsically addressed not to natural existing things but to ideal essences, poetic or logical terms which thought may define and play with. When fortune or necessity diverts our attention from this congenial ideal sport to crude facts and pressing issues, we turn our frail poetic ideas into symbols for those terrible irruptive things. In that paper money of our own stamping, the legal tender of the mind, we are obliged to reckon all the movements and values of the world.

The universal American I speak of is one of these symbols; and I should be still speaking in symbols and creating moral units and a false simplicity, if I spoke of classes pedantically sub-divided, or individuals ideally integrated and defined. As it happens, the symbolic American can be made largely adequate to the facts; because, if there are immense differences between individual Americans—for some Americans are black—yet there is a great uniformity in their environment, customs, temper, and thoughts. They have all been uprooted from their several soils and ancestries and plunged together into one vortex, whirling irresistibly in a space otherwise quite empty. To be an American is of itself almost a moral condition, an education, and a career. Hence a single ideal figment can cover a large part of what each American is in his character, and almost the whole of what most Americans are in their social outlook and political judgments.

The discovery of the new world exercised a sort of selection among the inhabitants of Europe. All the colonists, except the negroes, were voluntary exiles. The fortunate, the deep-rooted, and the lazy remained at home; the wilder instincts or dissatisfaction of others tempted them beyond the horizon. The American is accordingly the most adventurous, or the descendant of the most adventurous, of Europeans. It is in his blood to be socially a radical, though perhaps not intellectually. What has existed in the past, especially in the remote past, seems to him not only not authoritative, but irrelevant, inferior and outworn. He finds it rather a sorry waste of time to think about the past at all. But his enthusiasm for the future is profound; he can conceive of no more decisive way of recommending an opinion or a practice than to say that it is what everybody is coming to adopt. This expectation of what he approves or approval of what he expects makes up his optimism. It is the necessary faith of the pioneer.

Such a temperament is of course not maintained in the nation merely by inheritance. Inheritance notoriously tends to restore the average of a race and plays incidentally many a trick of atavism. What maintains the temperament and makes it national is social contagion or pressure—something immensely strong in democracies. The luckless American who happens to be born a conservative, or who is drawn to poetic subtlety, pious retreats, or gay passions, nevertheless has the categorical excellence of work, growth, enterprise, reform, and prosperity dinned into his ears; every door is open in this direction and shut in the other; so that he either folds up his heart and withers in a corner—in remote places you sometimes find such a solitary gaunt idealist —or else he flies to Oxford or Florence or Montmartre to save his soul—or perhaps not to save it.

The optimism of the pioneer is not limited to his view of himself and his own future; it starts from that; but feeling assured, safe, and cheery within, he looks with smiling and most kindly eyes on everything and everybody about him. Individualism, roughness, and self-trust are supposed to go with selfishness and a cold heart, but I suspect that is a prejudice. It is rather dependence, insecurity, and mutual jostling, that poison our placid gregarious brotherhood; and fanciful passionate demands upon people's affections, when they are disappointed, as they soon must be, breed ill-will and a final meanness. The milk of human kindness is less apt to turn sour if the vessel that holds it stands steady, cool and separate, and is not too often uncorked. In his affections the American is seldom passionate, often deep, and always kindly. If it were given me to look into the depths of a man's heart, and I did not find goodwill at the bottom, I should say without any hesitation: you are not an American. But as the American is an individualist his goodwill is not officious. His instinct is to think well of everybody, and to wish everybody well, but in a spirit of rough comradeship, expecting every man to stand on his own legs and to be helpful in his turn. When he has given his neighbour a chance he thinks he has done enough for him; but he feels it is an absolute duty to do that. It will take some hammering to drive a coddling socialism into America.

As self-trust may pass into self-sufficiency, so optimism, kindness and goodwill may grow into a general habit of doting on everything. To the good American many subjects are sacred; sex is sacred, women are sacred, children are sacred, business is sacred, America is sacred, Masonic lodges and college clubs are sacred. This feeling grows out of the good opinion he wishes to have of these things, and serves to maintain it. If he did not regard all these things as sacred he might come to doubt sometimes if they were wholly good. Of this kind too is the idealism of single ladies in reduced circumstances who can see the soul of beauty in ugly things, and are perfectly happy because their old dog has such pathetic eyes, their minister is so eloquent, their garden with its three sun-flowers is so pleasant, their dead friends were so devoted, and their distant relations are so rich.

Consider now the great emptiness of America, not merely the primitive physical emptiness, surviving in some regions, and the continental spacing of the chief natural features, but also the moral emptiness of a settlement where men and even houses are easily moved about and on one, almost, lives where he was born or believes what he has been taught. Not that the American has jettisoned these impedimenta in anger; they have simply slipped from him as he moves. Great empty spaces bring a sort of freedom to both soul and body. You may pitch your tent where you will; or if ever you decide to build anything, it can be in a style of your own devising. You have room, fresh materials, few models, and no critics. You trust your own experience, not only because you must, but because you find you may do so safely and prosperously; the forces that determine fortune are not yet too complicated for one man to explore. Your detachable condition makes you lavish with money and cheerfully experimental; you lose little if you lose all, since you remain completely yourself. At the same time your absolute initiative gives you practice in coping with novel situations, and in being original; it teaches you shrewd management. Your life and mind will become dry and direct, with few decorative flourishes. In your works everything will be stark and pragmatic; you will not understand why anybody should make those little sacrifices to instinct or custom which we call grace. The fine arts will seem to you academic luxuries, fit to amuse the ladies, like Greek and Sanskrit; for while you will perfectly appreciate generosity in men's purposes, you will not admit that the execution of these purposes can be anything but business. Unfortunately the essence of the fine arts is that the execution should be generous too, and delightful in itself; therefore the fine arts will suffer, not so much in their express professional pursuit—for then they become practical tasks and a kind of business—as in that diffused charm which qualifies all human action when men are artists by nature. Elaboration, which is something to accomplish, will be preferred to simplicity, which is something to rest in; manners will suffer somewhat; speech will suffer horribly. For the American the urgency of his novel attack upon matter, his zeal in gathering its fruits, precludes meanderings in primrose paths; means must be economical, and symbols must be mere symbols. If his wife wants luxuries, of course she may have them, and if he has vices, that can be provided for him too; but they must all be set down under those headings in his books.

At the same time the American is imaginative; for where life is intense, imagination is intense also. Were he not imaginative he would not live so much in the future. But his imagination is practical and the future it forecasts is immediate; it works with the clearest and least ambiguous terms known to his experience, in terms of number, measure, contrivance, economy, and speed. He is an idealist working on matter. Understanding as he does the material potentialities of things, he is successful in invention, conservative in reform, and quick in emergencies. All his life he jumps into the train after it has started and jumps out before it has stopped and he never once gets left behind or breaks a leg. There is an enthusiasm in his sympathetic handling of material forces which goes far to cancel the illiberal character which it might otherwise assume. The good workman hardly distinguishes his artistic intention from the potency in himself and in things which are about to realize that intention. Accordingly his ideals fall into the form of premonition and prophecies; and his studious prophecies often come true. So do the happy workmanlike ideals of the American. When a poor boy, perhaps he dreams of an education, and presently he gets an education, or at least a degree: he dreams of growing rich, and he grows rich—only more slowly and modestly, perhaps, than he expected; he dreams of marrying his Rebecca, and even if he marries a Leah instead, he ultimately finds in Leah his Rebecca after all. He dreams of helping to carry on and to accelerate the movement of a vast, seething, progressive society, and he actually does so. Ideals clinging so close to nature are almost sure of fulfillment. The American beams with a certain self-confidence and sense of mastery; he feels that God and nature are working with him.

In America there is a tacit optimistic assumption about existence, to the effect that the more existence the better. The soul-less critic might urge that quantity is but a physical category, implying no excellence, but at best an abundance of opportunities both for good and for evil. But the young soul, being curious and hungry, views existence *a priori* under the form of the good: its instinct to live implies a faith that most things it can become or see or do will be worth while. Respect for quantity is accordingly something more than the childish joy and wonder at bigness: it is the fisherman's joy in a big haul, the good uses of which he can take for granted. Such optimism is amiable. Nature cannot afford that we should begin by being too calculating or wise, and she encourages us by the pleasure she attaches to our functions in advance of their fruits, and often in excess of them; as the angler enjoys catching his fish more than eating it, and often waiting patiently for the fish to bite misses his own supper. The pioneer must devote himself to preparations; he must work for the future, and it is healthy and dutiful of him to love his work for its own sake. At the same time unless reference to an ultimate purpose is at least virtual in all his activities, he runs the danger of becoming a living automaton, vain and ignominious in its mechanical constancy. Idealism about work can hide an intense materialism about life. Man, if he is a rational being, cannot live by bread alone nor be a labourer merely: he must eat and work in view of an ideal harmony which overarches all his days, and which is realized in the way they hang together or in some ideal issue which they have in common. Otherwise, though his technical philosophy may call itself idealism, he is a materialist in morals: he esteems things, and esteems himself, for mechanical uses and energies. Even sensualists, artists, and pleasure-lovers are wiser than that, for though their idealism may be desultory or corrupt, they attain something ideal, and prize things only for their living effects, moral though perhaps fugitive. Sensation, as I have already suggested, when we do not take it as a signal for action, but arrest and peruse what it positively brings before us, reveals something ideal—a colour, shape, or sound; and to dwell on these presences, with no thought of their material significance, is an aesthetic or dreamful idealism. To pass from this idealism to the knowledge of matter is a great intellectual advance, and goes with dominion over the world; for in the practical arts the mind is adjusted to a larger object, with more depth and potentiality in it; which is what makes people feel that the material world is real, as they call it, and that the ideal world is not. Certainly the material world is real; for the philosophers who deny the existence of matter are like the critics who deny the existence of Homer: if there was never any Homer there must have been a lot of other poets no less Homeric than he; and if matter does not exist, a combination of other things exists which is just as material. But the intense reality of the material world would not prevent it from being a dreary waste in our eyes, or even an abyss of horror, if it brought forth no spiritual fruits. In fact it does bring forth spiritual fruits, for otherwise we should not be here to find fault with it, and to set up our ideals over against it. Nature is material, but not materialistic; it issues in life, and breeds all sorts of warm passions and idle beauties. And just as sympathy with the mechanical travail and turmoil of nature, apart from its spiritual fruits, is moral materialism, so the continual perception and love of these fruits is moral idealism—happiness in the presence of immaterial objects and harmonies, such as we envisage in affection, speculation, religion, and all the forms of the beautiful.

The circumstances of his life hitherto have necessarily driven the American into moral materialism: for in his dealings with material things he can hardly stop to enjoy their sensible aspects, which are ideal, nor proceed at once to their ultimate uses, which are ideal too. He is practical as against the poet, and worldly as against the clear philosopher or the saint. The most striking expression of this materialism is usually supposed to be his love of the almighty dollar; but that is a foreign and unintelligent view. The American talks about money, because that is the symbol and measure he has at hand for success, intelligence, and power; but as to money itself he makes, loses, spends, and gives it away with a very light heart. To my mind the most striking expression of his materialism is his singular preoccupation with quantity. If, for instance, you visit Niagara Falls, you may expect to hear how many cubic feet or metric tons of water are precipitated per second over the cataract; how many cities and towns (with the number of their inhabitants) derive light and motive power from it; and the annual value of the further industries that might very well be carried on by the same means, without visibly depleting the world's greatest wonder or injuring the tourist trade. That is what I confidently expected to hear on arriving at the adjoining town of Buffalo: but I was deceived. The first thing I heard instead was that there are more miles of asphalt pavement in Buffalo than in any city in the world.

Nor is this insistence on quantity confined to men of business. The President of Harvard College, seeing me once by chance soon after the beginning of a term, inquired how my classes were getting on; and when I replied that I thought they were getting on well, that my men seemed to be keen and intelligent, he stopped me as if I was about to waste his time; "I meant," said he, "I meant *what is the number* of students in your classes."

Here I think we may perceive that this love of quantity often has a silent partner, which is diffidence as to quality. The democratic conscience recoils before anything that savours of privilege; and lest it should concede an unmerited privilege to any pursuit or person, it reduces all things as far as possible to the common denominator of quantity. Numbers cannot lie; but if it came to comparing the ideal beauties of philosophy with those of Anglo-Saxon, who should decide? All studies are good—why else have universities?—but those must be most encouraged which attract the greatest number of students. Hence the President's question. Democratic faith, in its diffidence about quality, throws the reins of education on the pupil's neck, as Don Quixote threw the reins on the neck of Rocinante, and bids his divine instinct choose its own way.

The American has never yet had to face the trials of Job. Great crises, like the Civil War, he has known how to surmount victoriously; and when he has surmounted the present crisis victoriously also, it is possible that he may relapse, as he did in the other case, into an apparently complete absorption in material enterprise and prosperity. But if serious and irremediable tribulation ever overtook him, what would his attitude be? It is then that we should be able to discover whether materialism or idealism lies at the base of his character. Meantime his working mind is not without its holiday. He spreads humour pretty thick and even over the surface of conversation, and humour is one form of moral emancipation. He loves landscape, he loves mankind, and he loves knowledge; and in music at least he finds an art which he unfeignedly enjoys. In music and landscape, in humour and kindness, he touches the ideal more truly, perhaps, than in his ponderous academic idealisms, and busy religions—for it is astonishing how much even religion in America (can it possibly be so in England?) is a matter of meetings, building-funds, schools, charities, clubs, and picnics. To be poor in order to be simple, to produce less, in order that the product may be more choice and beautiful, and may leave us less burdened with unnecessary duties and useless possessions—that is an ideal not articulate in the American mind; yet here and there I seem to have heard a sigh after it, a groan at the perpetual incubus of business and shrill society. What does it profit a man to free the whole world, if his soul is not free? Moral freedom is not an artificial condition, because the ideal is the mother-tongue of both the heart and the senses. All that is requisite is that we should pause in living to enjoy life, and should lift up our hearts to things that are pure goods in themselves, so that once to have found and loved them, whatever else may betide, may be a happiness that nothing can sully. This natural idealism does not imply that we are immaterial, but only that we are animate and truly alive. When the senses are sharp and joyous, as in the American, they are already half liberated; and when the heart is warm, like his, and eager to be just, its ideal destiny is hardly doubtful. Time and its own pulses will give it wings.

Marginal Notes on Civilization
in the United States

One of the notable publishing events in 1922, a remarkably productive year in literary and cultural history, was the appearance of *Civilization in the United States: An Inquiry by Thirty Americans*, a symposium edited by Harold E. Stearns. A sampling of its contributors and topics will suggest its range and point of view: Lewis Mumford on The City, H. L. Mencken on Politics, Robert Morse Lovett on Education, J. E. Spingarn on Scholarship and Criticism, and Van Wyck Brooks on The Literary Life. Its tone is uniformly and sharply critical, and its spirit of liberation is symbolized in the self-consciously inscribed dateline to the editor's Preface: "New York City, July Fourth, 1921." As this preface makes clear, the symposium is anti-genteel tradition, which is doubtless what moved the editors of the *Dial* to ask Santayana to review it, his own critique of American civilization having appeared two years earlier. The article that resulted, "Marginal Notes on Civilization in the United States," may well have shocked the editors and readers of the *Dial* because it is ill-tempered and largely unsympathetic. Having little affection for the genteel tradition, Santayana appears here to have had even less for "reformism" and a horror of what he seems to have regarded as its political concomitant, "bolshevism." The decidedly cranky tone of these "marginal notes" provides a valuable corrective to the easy misconception that this very stimulating critic of American culture was democratic or progressive or modern—adjectives which, if applied to himself, he would have disliked and disclaimed.

"Marginal Notes on Civilization in the United States" is reprinted from the *Dial*, 72 (June 1922).

Title Page

What is Civilization? Porcelain bath-tubs, et cetera? Fine art? Free thought? Virtue? Peace? Peace, virtue, and free thought might exist in Arcadia or in the Islands of the Blest, neither of which would be called exactly civilized. Civilized means citified, trained, faithful to some regimen deliberately instituted. Civilization might be taken as a purely descriptive term, like *Kultur*, rather than as a eulogistic one; it might simply indicate the possession of instruments, material and social, for accomplishing all sorts of things, whether those things were worth accomplishing or not. If we insist on taking civilization as a term of praise, we must mean by it something like institutions making for the highest happiness; and what such happiness is could not be defined without plunging into moral philosophy, in which no two persons would agree.

Contents

The list of the thirty American authors of this book, and the three foreigners, makes me tremble. I know a good many of them and some (though this is not the moment to boast of it) have been my pupils. I foresee that I am to hear the plaints of superior and highly critical minds, suffering from maladaptation; and that I shall learn more about their palpitating doubts than about America or about civilization. Nevertheless, as they are a part of America—although they may forget to give America credit for having produced them—I shall be learning something about America after all; and if their strictures upon their country sadden me, I can always comfort myself with a fact which they may be too modest to notice; namely, that civilization can't be at a low ebb where thirty such spirits can be brought together in a jiffy, by merely whistling for them.

Preface

"As long ago as the autumn of last year . . . we wished to take advantage of the strategic situation . . . decided . . . by majority vote . . . to be good-natured and . . . urbane . . . No martyrs, and no one who was merely disgruntled . . . Slow and careful selection . . . of likeminded men and women . . . in common defense against . . . reaction." Quite as I thought. Indignation at the powers that be is a frequent source of eloquence in Europe; I have not known it before in America on this scale. I shall be all ears.

Page vi. *"There is a sharp dichotomy between preaching and practice; we let not our right hand know what our left hand doeth . . . The moral code resolves itself into . . . fear of what people will say."* I see the fact which Mr Stearns points to here, but not as he sees it. The American conscience is not insincere; it is only belated, inapplicable. The sanctities are traditional; sentiment preserves and requires the habits and language of an elder age; it has all the sincerity of instinct. But it does not exactly fit the exigences of public life, which has been transformed and accelerated in a way which conscience can't keep up with, yet is dazzled by and has not the heart to condemn; for it has to keep house, as it were, with an obstreperous younger brother, the conscience of emancipated human nature, with its new set of illusions and its pride in its thundering, pushing life. The American intellect is shy and feminine; it paints nature in water-colours; whereas the sharp masculine eye sees the world as a moving-picture—rapid, dramatic, vulgar, to be glanced at and used merely as a sign of what is going to happen next. Mere man in America hardly has an articulate logic in which to express his practical convictions, and I doubt if even this book will supply the want. I won't say that it is itself genteel; that would enrage its revolutionary authors too much; they may have forgotten that Emerson and Thoreau and Brook Farm were revolutionary. But if not genteel and not specifically American, the spirit of these critics is one of offended sensibility. Things shock them; and their compensatory ideals and plans of reform are fetched from abstract reflection or irrelevant enthusiasms. They are far from expressing the manly heart of America, emancipated from the genteel tradition. They seem to be morally underfed, and they are disaffected

Page vii. *"American civilization is . . . not Anglo-Saxon. . . . Until we begin . . . to cherish the heterogeneous elements which make up our life . . . we shall remain . . . a polyglot boarding-house."* M Doumic, a French observer, has said that, while the English and Germans are races, the United States, like France, is a *milieu*—what American philosophy calls a "situation." Only in France the memory and discipline of past situations survives in the different classes and parties, in the church, army, government, and literature; whereas in America, apart from a rather pale genteel tradition, only the present situation counts. It is the present task, the present state of business, and present fashion in pleasure that create the hearty unity and universal hum of America—just the unity which these thirty individualists resent, and wish to break up. Why not be patient? Situations change quickly. Why not enjoy moral variety *seriatim* instead of simultaneously? A proof that Americanism is the expression of a present material environment, is that the immigrants at once feel themselves and actually become typical Americans, more instinct with an aggressive Americanism than the natives of Cape Cod or the poor whites in the South. Another consequence is that the whole world is being Americanized by the telephone, the trolley car, the department store, and the advertising press. Americanism, apart from the genteel tradition, is simply modernism—purer in America than elsewhere because less impeded and qualified by survivals of the past, but just as pure in Spanish-Italian Buenos Aires as in Irish-Jewish New York. If by cherishing heterogeneous elements, Mr Stearns means preserving the foreign nationalities in the new environment, I am afraid it is impossible. A leading German whom I questioned on this subject (before the war) assured me that in New York he could not prevail on his children to speak German at home, nor to keep up any German traditions. The contagion and rush of the *milieu* are too strong.

Page vii. "*The mania for petty regulation, the driving, regimentating, and drilling, the secret society and its grotesque regalia, the ... material organization of our pleasures and gaieties ... painted devils ... to frighten us away from the acknowledgment of our spiritual poverty.*" It is not so bad as that, not at all Satanic. There ought to have been a chapter in this book on manners and social intercourse. The heartiness of American ways, the feminine gush and the masculine go, the girlishness and high jinks and perpetual joking and obligatory jollity may prove fatiguing sometimes; but children often overdo their sports, which does not prove that they are not spontaneous fundamentally. Social intercourse is essentially play, a kind of perpetual amiable comedy; the relish of it comes of liking our part and feeling we are doing it nicely, and that the others are playing up as they should. The atmosphere of sport, fashion, and wealth is agreeable and intoxicating; certainly it is frivolous, unless some passion is at work beneath, and even then it is all vanity; but in that sense, so is life itself, and a philosopher who is really a philosopher will not quarrel with it on that account. What else than vanity could life possibly be in the end? The point is that it should be spontaneous, innocent, and happily worked out, like a piece of music well-played. Isn't American life distinctly successful in expressing its own spirit?

The City

Page 9-11. *"The highest achievements of our material civilization . . . count as so many symptoms of its spiritual failure . . . escape from the environment . . . exotic architecture . . ."* It is the common fate of all Christendom that, being based on revolution and barbarian recalcitrancy, it has a divided mind. Its arts cannot proceed ingenuously in a straight line of development, but must struggle on by revivals, adaptations, archaisms, and abortions. I think architecture in America is most promising: the architects are intelligent and well-informed; they are beginning to be prudent; and public taste is very watchful and discriminating. It is not in churches nor in great official edifices that artistic success or originality can be expected, but rather in engineering works, such as sky-scrapers, or else in ordinary private houses, such as in England are called cottages and in America "Homes." Shaded streets of detached villas, each in its pocket-handkerchief of land, are distinctively American. With a little more solidity in the materials and a little more repose in the designs, they might be wholly pleasing; and if sometimes they seem chaotic and flimsy, as if they were a row of band-boxes laid on the ground and not houses built of foundations, perhaps they only express the better the shifting population which they shelter. They are the barracks of industrialism, which cannot live in the country, but is spilled out of the towns.

Politics

Page 21. [A representative . . . shall be an inhabitant of that state in which he shall be chosen.] *"Find me the worst ass in Congress, and I'll show you a man [whom this regulation has] helped to get there and to stay there. Find me the most shameless scoundrel, and I'll show you another."* I do not think this regulation is at fault; fair representatives might have been chosen by lot like jurymen. The trouble is that salaries, patronage, and the possibility of re-election have turned them into professional politicians. These are just as bad when attached to a national machine as to a local one. Representatives should merely interrupt their private business, during parts of two years when Congress is in session, and then return to the plough, the counter, or the work-shop. At the next election, someone else should be chosen to represent the interests and express the views of his fellow-citizens. In this way government by the people would not perish from the earth.

Page 23. *"The average congressman . . . is . . . not only incompetent and imbecile, but also incurably dishonest."*

Why exaggerate? *"His knowledge is that of a third-rate country lawyer . . . his intelligence is that of a country-newspaper editor, or evangelical divine. His standards of honour are those of a country banker . . ."* Why not? Shouldn't a representative be representative? A reformer, a prophet, an expert, a revolutionary committee sitting in enlightened New York would not be a fair vehicle of popular government. Isn't democracy built on the experience and the conviction that superior people are dangerous, and that the instinct of the common people is a safer guide? But what surprises me more than disbelief in democracy, is this hatred of the countryside. Is agriculture the root of evil? Naturally, the first rays of the sun must strike the east side of New York, but do they never travel beyond?

Journalism

Page 43. *"I fail to find any evidence of widespread disgust with the newspaper as it is."* Is it worse than the gossip diffused in the old days by barbers and porters? A racy popular paper is like the grave-digger in Hamlet, and I don't blame the people for paying a penny for it.

Pages 45-48. *"All newspapers are controlled by the advertising department . . . Business is behind government and government is behind business . . . It is a partnership of swindle."* Would it be better if government strove to ruin business and business to discredit government? And if government is stable and business prosperous, how is the nation swindled?

Pages 49-50. *"False 'optimism' . . . about the military exploits of Russia's enemies . . . Kolchak and Denekin . . . 'Lying about Lenin' goes merrily on . . . The London La-*

bour Herald exposed the trick of Lloyd George . . . the prince of political liars . . . Mr. Hughes' idiotic . . . attitude." This fairly lets the cat out of the bag. Mr Macy's objection to the American press is not that it is controlled by business or government, but only that this business is capitalistic and this government not a Soviet Republic.

Education

Page 77. "*Faith . . . in what is called education.*" Mr Lovett calls this the great American superstition, but appears to have great hopes of it himself, if it could only be directed to spreading enlightenment instead of prejudice. With "management of institutions of teaching by the teachers" (which he oddly calls democratic control) "the spoliation of the schools by politicians, the sacrifice of education to propaganda, the tyranny of the hierarchy can be successfully resisted." Page 91. But wouldn't a guild of teachers form an irresponsible hierarchy, imposing their ideas on society when they agreed, and quarrelling among themselves when they did not? If this syndicated enlightenment were simply offered without being imposed, people would go to school only as they go to the dentist, when aching for knowledge; and how often would that be? Freedom—and young America furnishes a proof of this—does not make for enlightenment; it makes for play. A free society would create sports, feasts, religion, poetry, music; its enlightenment would be confined to a few scattered sages, as in antiquity. What brings enlightenment is experience, in the sad sense of this word—the pressure of hard facts and unintelligible troubles, making a man rub his eyes in his waking dream, and put two and two together. Enlightenment is cold water. Education is quite another matter. "The purpose of this college," I heard the Master of Balliol say in 1887, "is to rear servants to the Queen." Education is the transmission of a moral and intellectual tradition, with its religion, manners, sentiments, and loyalties. It is not the instruction given in American schools and colleges that matters much, or that constitutes an American education; what matters is the tradition of alacrity, inquisitiveness, self-trust, spontaneous co-operation and club-spirit; all of which can ripen, in the better minds, into openness to light and fidelity to duty. The test of American education is not whether it produces enlightenment, but whether it produces competence and public well-being. Mr Lovett does not seem to remember that mankind is a tribe of animals, living by habit and thinking in symbols, and that it can never be anything else. If American education does not transmit such a perfect human discipline as that of a Greek city or of the British upper classes, that is not its fault; it works on a vaster canvas with thinner pigments. But its defect lies in not being thoroughly and deeply enough the very thing which Mr Lovett condemns it for being—a transmitted life.

Scholarship and Criticism

Page 94. *"Spiritual starvation . . . signs of its restless gnawing on the face of almost any American woman beyond the first flush of youth . . . hopeless craving on the face of almost any mature American man."*

Page 98. *"Body but no soul . . . freshness is not there . . . scholars without scholarship . . . churches without religion."* What can be the cause of this dreadful state of things? There are just three causes: Page 101 (1) *"The conception of literature as a moral influence"*; (2) *"The . . . conception of literature as the . . . vehicle for a new 'Weltanschauung'"*; (3) *"The conception of . . . 'art for art's sake.'"* And there are just three remedies to be applied: Page 105 (1) "*Aesthetic thinking . . . The haphazard empiricism of English criticism and the faded moralism of our own will serve us no more . . . We must seek purer and deeper streams . . . Only in this way can we gain what America lacks, the brain-illumined soul.*" (2) "*Knowledge . . . a wider international outlook and a deeper national insight*"; (3) "*Training in taste . . . a more complete submission to the imaginative will of the artist.*" My own experience does not suggest that Americans are wanting in taste, knowledge, or aesthetic thinking; on the contrary, a great preoccupation and anxiety about these things, a thirst for culture and a desire not to miss or misunderstand anything, seem to be a chief part of their spiritual misery. They are perpetually troubled lest they should not fully enjoy the morning sunshine and their delicious oatmeal and cream and cubist painting and the poetry of Miss Amy Lowell; while their love for Botticelli is a tender passion and their preference for Michael Angelo over Raphael is a philosophic conviction. I hardly think that if the aesthetics of Hegel and of Croce were taught in the high schools the facial muscles of the nation would relax and they would burst into passionate song, like Neapolitan minstrels. What I should like somebody to explain is the American voice and language and newspapers; where taste and sensibility are hardened to such a pervasive ugliness (or else affectation) in these familiar things, it is needless to look further for the difficulties which beset the artist, in spite of his high ambitions and enlightenment. The artistic idiom is foreign to him; he cannot be simple, he cannot be unconscious, he has no native, unquestioned, inevitable masters. And it is not easy for native masters to spring up; the moral soil is too thin and shifting, like sand in an hour-glass, always on the move; whatever traditions there are, practical man and reformers insist on abandoning; every house is always being pulled down for rebuilding; nothing can take root; nothing can be assumed as a common affection, a common pleasure; no refinement of sense, no pause, no passion, no candour, no enchantment. The thirty authors of this book, for instance, give out that they are the salt of the nation: "We have a vitality and nervous alertness," they say (page 149) "which . . . might cut through the rocks of stupidity . . . Our cup of life is full to the brim," and I have no reason to doubt it. Yet none of them seems ever to have loved anything; that cup must be filled with a very unpalatable liquid; and this is how they write: "scheme of undergraduate emphases, grouped and amended as his triumphant progress permitted him to check up on his observations." "A curtailment of potential scientific achievement through the general deficiencies of the cultural environment." "Little of this talent succeeds in effectuating itself." "The fountain-pen with which a great poem is written." "Producing and buying art." "This is not postured for sensational effect." "Essayed to boo it into permanent discard." "Arrived at a degree of theatrical polish sufficient to boast a little playhouse up an ulterior mews.'" "Sex, save it be presented in terms of a seltzer-siphon, 'Abendstern,' or the *Police Gazette,* spells failure." "Exceptions portend the first signs of the coming dawn." "Formulaic crisis-psychology." "Too little faith in the rationality of the collect to believe that problems can be faced in battalions." "Let a producer break away from the mantel-leaning histrionism and palm-pot investiture, and against him is brought up the curt dismissal of freakishness." "Scarcely time to admire a millionth part . . . before a new and greatly improved universe floats across the horizon and, from every corner news-stand, smilingly bids us enter its portals." Indeed there is scarcely time; and I should be sorry to seem to break away with the curt dismissal of freakishness, but I can't help agreeing with what I have marked on another page, that "our ways of expression are very wasteful" and that "when these rebels really begin to think, the confusion is increased."

School and College Life

Page 109. "*American . . . cities are only less identical than the trains that ply between them.*" Yes; when I went to California I discovered that West Newton, Mass., extends to the Pacific. Page 112. "*Americans are . . . uniformly charming.*" In intention they are; they come forward smiling, "happy to meet you," and apparently confident that the happiness will be mutual; they beam as if sure to charm; but are they uniformly charming in fact? Charm seems to rest on something more than conventional kindness and effusiveness, on subtle gifts which are not voluntary. Page 113. "*If our convictions . . . sprang from real knowledge of ourselves and of our capacities, we should relish egoists, disinterested critics, intellectuals, artists, and irreverent humorists.*" Each such person would relish himself, even if they did not relish one another. But Americans are diffident, often feigning an assurance which they are far from feeling, and not able heartily to snap their fingers at public opinion. The instinct and the ideal of uniformity are very profound in them; if they are compelled to be rebels, they become propagandists, like the authors of this book, and if they cannot conform to the majority they are not happy until they make the majority conform to them. Why this passion? Page 114. The teacher is "*a harassed young woman . . . who has to answer, or silence, the questions of from a score to three score mouths. So begins that long throttling of curiosity which later on will baffle the college instructor.*" This is an effect of being taught in classes; we listen to the droning recitation or lecture as to the patter of rain. I believe in schools, especially in boarding-schools and colleges, because I think they are good for the character, and a relief to the family and from the family; but they are bad for the intellect. A spark, no doubt, will fly occasionally from the teacher and kindle some thought or interest in the pupil; but he must depend for stimulus on what he can pick up from books and from casual contacts. Fortunately the school or college gives him intellectual leisure and space, and allows him to brood; so that if there is intellect enough in him to be worth asserting, it can assert itself. Page 116. *"The American undergraduate is representative of the American temper at its best . . . As he thinks and feels, all America would think and feel if it dared and could."* Yes; and what an immense improvement it would be! The undergraduate is not devoted to making money; he is not subject to women; he does, except when the pressure or fear of the outer world constrains him, only what he finds worth doing for its own sake. I wish reformers, instead of trying to make the colleges more useful and professional, would try to make the world more like the colleges. The things that the world might find worth doing for their own sake would perhaps be nobler than those that appeal to the undergraduate, though I am far from confident of that; but in any case, means would no longer be pursued as ends. The world would then shine with what is called honour, which is allegiance to what one knows one loves.

Science

Page 151. *"In art . . . mediocrity is worthless and incapable of giving inspiration to genius. But in science . . . every bit of sound work . . . counts."* It counts in art also, when art is alive. In a thoroughly humanized society everything—clothes, speech, manners, government—is a work of art, being so done as to be a pleasure and a stimulus in itself. There seems to be an impression in America that art is fed on the history of art, and is what is found in museums. But museums are mausoleums, only dead art is there, and only ghosts of artists flit about them. The priggish notion that an artist is a person undertaking to produce immortal works suffices to show that art has become a foreign thing, an *hors-d'œuvre,* and that it is probably doomed to affectation and sterility. Page 155. *"American science . . . is . . . a hothouse growth."* I am surprised to hear this, as I supposed that astronomy, chemistry, natural history, and medicine were nowhere more at home. That science may have practical applications, or even may be pursued in view of them, does not seem to me to militate against its scientific purity, nor against a pure enthusiasm for knowledge. It is again as in art; the thrill, the vision, the happy invention come to the faithful workman as a free gift, in the midst of his labour.

The Literary Life

Page 180. *"The chronic state of our literature is that of a youthful promise which is never redeemed."* The fate of the Harvard poets in my time—Sanborn, McCulloch, Stickney, Lodge, Savage, Moody—was a tragic instance of this. If death had not cut them all off prematurely, would they have fulfilled their promise? I think that Moody, who actually accomplished most, would have succeeded notably, in that as a dramatist or as a poet with a mission, he would have secured general attention and respect; but even so, it might have been at the expense of his early poetic colour and disinterested passion for beauty. Stickney, who was the one I knew best, could never, I am sure, have prospered in the American air. Although he was a Harvard man, he had been well taught privately first, and afterwards for many years studied in Paris. When he returned to Harvard to teach Greek, he was heroically determined to take the thing seriously, and to share enthusiastically the life of his country; but the instrument was far too delicate and sensitive for the work; his imaginative (yet exact) learning, his spiritual ardour, his remote allegiances (as for instance to Indian philosophy) could not have survived the terrible inertia and the more terrible momentum of his new environment. Not that America does not afford material opportunities and even stimulus for the intellectual life, provided it is not merely retrospective or poetical; a man like William James, whose plough could cut into rough new ground, left an indelible furrow; but he had a doctor's healthy attitude towards human ills, his Pragmatism was a sort of diagnosis of America, and even he would have found it uphill work to cultivate beauty of form, to maintain ultimate insights, or to live in familiar friendship with the Greeks and the Indians. I managed it after a fashion myself, because I was conscious of being a foreigner with my essential breathing tubes to other regions; nor did I really belong to the irritable genus; I had perhaps more natural stamina, less fineness, more unconcern, and the spirit of mockery, in the last resort, to protect me.

Music

Page 210. *"The American composer . . . works more or less in a vacuum. He is out of things and he knows it."* Why should he mind that? Music is a world above the worlds, and the ladder into it can be planted anywhere. I suspect the difficulty lies in a divided allegiance: the musician will not live on music alone, he is no true musician. Snobbery, the anxiety to succeed, and a sort of cowardly social instinct stand between the artist and his work. It is because he wants "to be in things" that he fails, and deserves to fail.

Economic Opinion

Page 255. *"The idea that knowledge . . . is essential to the right to an opinion . . . is little understood here."* Because opinions are regarded as expressing people and not things. This is a consequence of modern philosophy, or the principle of it. All opinions are free and equal if, as modern philosophy maintains, they have no objects and are essentially opinions about nothing; the truth can then only be a harmony or a compromise established among these opinions. You shake the ballots in a hat, and pull out salvation.

Radicalism

Page 277. *"Radicalism arises neither from a . . . desire for more material goods, nor from . . . a particular formula . . . It arises from a desire to be free, to achieve dignity and independence . . . To be poor . . . is less annoying than to be moderately well paid while the man who fixes one's wages rides in a Rolls-Royce . . . You may challenge [the workman] to prove that any other system would work better . . . Reasoning will affect him little. He . . . wants . . . power."* If envy is the only motive making for a revolution, the revolution will not come except by force of a great delusion; because if the people *knew* that it would bring them no satisfaction but the satisfaction of envy, they would not want it. As to power, it is only the leaders who would have it, and would "ride in a Rolls-Royce" in the people's service; and accordingly it is only they who would profit by the revolution, since the satisfaction of envy is no benefit, but a new bitterness, like breaking another child's toys, you wanted those fine things for yourselves, and you have made them impossible for anybody. It is very characteristic of "radicalism" to boast in this way that it is unreasonable and mean and to ask you threateningly what you will do about it. For my own part, I can do nothing, except be very sorry for the radicals and for the people they would feed on the satisfaction of envy.

The Small Town

Page 296. *"There obviously cannot be among such a naturally healthy people a supercilious contempt for sentiment . . . We may listen to the band concert on a Saturday night in the Court House Square with a studied indifference . . . But deep down in our hearts is a feeling of invincible pride."* Here at last is a note of affection; also some rays of humour. Perhaps the extreme complacency about America that is characteristic of the majority, and the profound discomfort and shamefacedness of the minority, when it becomes critical, have a common root in the habit of thinking in terms of comparison, of perpetual competition; either a thing must be the biggest and best in the world, or you must blush for it. But only ways and means are good comparatively and on a single scale of values. Anything good intrinsically, anything loved for its own sake, is its own standard, and sufficient as it is. The habit of always comparing it with something else is impertinent and shallow. It betrays a mind that possesses nothing, loves nothing, and is nothing.

The Family

Pages 334-336. *"The asylums are . . . crowded . . . The groundwork for fatal ruptures . . . is laid . . . in the home*

. . . Parents . . . never entertain a modest doubt as to whether they might be the best of all possible company for their children . . . They need themselves to understand and practise the art of . . . happiness." The prevalence of insanity, of "breaking down," and of "nervous depression" is one of the most significant things in America. It goes with overwork, with not having a religion or "getting religion" (which is an incident to not having one) with absence of pleasures, forced optimism, routine, essential solitude. An intense family life would prevent all these miseries, but it would take away personal liberty. The modern family is only the egg-shell from which you are hatched; there you have your bed, clothes, meals, and relations; your life is what occupies you when you are out. But as you foregather only with chicks of your own age, who are as destitute as yourself, you remain without the moral necessaries. The test of a good school or college is its capacity to supply them. It is the only remaining spiritual home.

Advertising

Page 395. "*Outdoor advertising . . . should be removed from sight with all possible haste.*" A truly radical view. It is not to the eye only that America would be entirely transformed if a severe paternal government abolished advertising. The key of the whole symphony would be lowered, the soft pedal put on. Imagine the change in speed, if you were reduced to consulting your inner man before buying anything or going anywhere, and to discovering first whether you really wanted anything, and what it was! And imagine, when your inner need had become clear and peremptory all of itself, having to inquire of some shy official, or of some wise stranger, whether just the suit of clothes, or the play or the tour which your soul dreamt of could possibly be brought anywhere into the realm of fact, or must remain a dream for ever! It would not be often that geography or theatrical managers or tailors would have providentially anticipated your wishes, or would consent to realize them; so that your wants would soon be marvellously reduced and your soul chastened. But I suppose the idea of these radical reformers is that this very paternal government, in abolishing advertising, would supply you with such clothes and such dramas and such holiday excursions as you *ought* to want, and when you *ought* to want them. It would be a reversion to antiquity, to the pious peace and leisure of the most remote province in the most backward country. Personally I should have no objection; but is this the revolutionary ideal of "civilization in America"?

Business

Pages 413-414. "*Business is . . . blind . . . with extravagant reflex powers of accommodation and extension and almost no faculty of original imagination . . . It has brought about a marvellous economy of human effort. At the same time . . . it wastes the living machine in recurring periods of frightful and unnecessary idleness . . . It wastes the spirit . . . in the effort to create new and extravagant wants.*" Admirable summary; inventions and organization which ought to have increased leisure, by producing the necessaries with little labour, have only increased the population, degraded labour, and diffused luxury.

Sport and Play

Page 458. "*Its true . . . function is the cultivation of bodily vigour, with a view to longevity.*" Unless this is ironical—and I am sometimes in doubt how to interpret the style of these authors—it is an astonishingly illiberal thing to say. What is the use of longevity? If you said that the purpose of sport was health, that would come nearer the truth, because health at least suggests a *good* life, and is a part of what makes life worth having as it runs, which the length of life is not. The Greeks would have said that the purposes of gymnastics were beauty and military fitness; this too would be a more acceptable thing to say, since beauty and fitness for war and for victory contribute, like health, to the zest and dignity of existence, while existence lasts. But essentially sport has no purpose at all; it is an end in itself, a part of that free fruition of life which is the purpose of other things, when they are good for anything, and which, when present, can make a long life better than a short one. Its possible uses are incidental, like those of the fine arts, religion, or friendship. Not to see this is to be a barbarian.

Humour

Pages 463-466. *"Belief in American humour is a superstition . . . The prolongation of a single posture of the mind is intolerable . . . If by a happy stroke of fancy a cow in the dining-room is made pleasing to the mind . . . with the presentation of nine cows in nine dining-rooms it has changed to pain."* I agree that a perpetual search for the incongruous, even if it keeps us laughing mechanically, is empty and vulgar and disgusting in the end. It is a perpetual punning in images. And yet I feel that there is a genuine spirit of humour abroad in America, and that it is one of the best things there. The constant sense of the incongruous, even if artificially stimulated and found only in trivial things, is an admission that existence is absurd; it is therefore a liberation of the spirit over against this absurd world; it is a laughing liberation, because the spirit is glad to be free;

and yet it is not a scornful nor bitter liberation, because a world that lets us laugh at it and be free is after all a friendly world. We have no need to bear that serious grudge against it which we should be justified in bearing if it fooled us altogether, and tortured us by its absurdities instead of amusing us and making us spiritually free.

The Genteel Tradition at Bay

This essay is the last, albeit the best known, of Santayana's essays on the genteel tradition. It was occasioned by a flurry of literary skirmishes involving an insurgent (or counterinsurgent) band of "New Humanists," led by Irving Babbitt and Paul Elmer More. These traditionalists came forward in the late twenties to challenge and protest the direction and tendencies of the "modernists" who were beginning to dominate the American literary scene. In 1930, the Humanists brought out a symposium entitled *Humanism and America*, which provoked a pitched battle between themselves and such younger writers as Malcolm Cowley, Edmund Wilson, R. P. Blackmur, and Lewis Mumford. Santayana's reaction to this controversy was curious but characteristic. He declined to side with the modernists, in whose company he would have been uncomfortable, to say the least. Rather, he chose to brand the Humanists with the epithet of his own invention which had by this time become a searing iron: genteel tradition. Begun as a review of *Humanism and America* for J. Middleton Murry's *New Adelphi*, the essay (as Santayana remarked to Murry) got "involved in all sorts of side issues"[1] and finally ended in becoming the occasion for urging what Santayana calls "the moral adequacy of naturalism."

"The Genteel Tradition at Bay" is reprinted from the *Saturday Review of Literature*, VII:24, 25, 26 (1931), where it first appeared as a three-part essay. It was later revised and reprinted as a separate volume, *The Genteel Tradition at Bay* (New York: Charles Scribner's Sons, 1931).
The Genteel Tradition at Bay by George Santayana. Copyright 1931 CSS; renewal copyright © 1959 Old Colony Trust Company. Copyright 1931 Time, Inc.; renewal copyright © 1959 The Saturday Review of Literature.

I

Analysis of Modernity

Twenty years ago the genteel tradition in America seemed ready to melt gracefully into the active mind of the country. There were few misgivings about the perfect health and the all-embracing genius of the nation: only go full speed ahead and everything worth doing would ultimately get done. The churches and universities might have some pre-American stock in trade, but there was nothing stubborn or recalcitrant about them; they were happy to bask in the golden sunshine of plutocracy; and there was a feeling abroad— which I think reasonable—that wherever the organization of a living thing is materially perfected, there an appropriate moral and intellectual life will arise spontaneously. But the gestation of a native culture is necessarily long, and the new birth may seem ugly to an eye accustomed to some other form of excellence.

Will the new life ever be as beautiful as the old? Certain

[1] *The Letters of George Santayana,* ed. Daniel Cory (New York: Charles Scribner's Sons, 1955), p. 254.

too tender or too learned minds may refuse to credit it. Old
Harvard men will remember the sweet sadness of Professor
Norton. He would tell his classes, shaking his head with a
slight sigh, that the Greeks did not play football. In America
there had been no French cathedrals, no Venetian school of
painting, no Shakespeare, and even no gentlemen, but only
gentlemanly citizens. The classes laughed, because that re-
cital of home truths seemed to miss the humor of them. It
was jolly to have changed all that; and the heartiness of the
contrary current of life in everybody rendered those murmurs useless and a little ridiculous. In them the genteel
tradition seemed to be breathing its last. Now, however, the
worm has turned. We see it raising its head more admonish-
ingly than ever, darting murderous glances at its enemies,
and protesting that it is not genteel or antiquated at all, but
orthodox and immortal. Its principles, it declares, are classical, and its true name is Humanism.

The humanists of the Renaissance were lovers of Greek and
of good Latin, scornful of all that was crabbed, technical,
or fanatical: they were pleasantly learned men, free from
any kind of austerity, who, without quarrelling with Christian dogma, treated it humanly, and partly by tolerance and
partly by ridicule hoped to neutralize all its metaphysical
and moral rigor. Even when orthodoxy was reaffirmed in
the seventeenth century and established all our genteel
traditions, some humanistic leaven was mixed in; among
Protestants there remained a learned unrest and the ratio-
nalistic criticism of tradition; among Catholics a classical
eloquence draping everything in large and seemly folds, so
that nothing trivial, barbaric, or ugly should offend the
cultivated eye. But apart from such influences cast upon
orthodoxy, the humanists continued their own labors. Their

sympathy with mankind was not really universal, since it stopped short at enthusiasm, at sacrifice, at all high passion or belief; but they loved the more physical and comic aspects of life everywhere and all curious knowledge, especially when it could be turned against prevalent prejudices or abuses. They believed in the sufficient natural goodness of mankind, a goodness humanized by frank sensuality and a wink at all amiable vices; their truly ardent morality was all negative, and flashed out in their hatred of cruelty and oppression and in their scorn of imposture. This is still the temper of revolutionaries everywhere, and of philosophers of the extreme Left. These, I should say, are more truly heirs to the humanists than the merely academic people who still read, or pretend to read, the classics, and who would like to go on thrashing little boys into writing Latin verses.

Greek and Roman studies were called the humanities because they abstracted from Christian divinity; and it was for this paganizing or humanizing value that they were loved; much as Platonism is espoused by some theologians, because it enables them to preserve a metaphysical moralism independent of that historic religious faith of which they are secretly ashamed. The humanist would not deserve his name if he were not in sympathy with the suppressed sides of human nature (sometimes, as today perhaps, the highest sides of it); and he must change his aversions as the ruling convention changes its idols. Thus hatred of exact logic, of asceticism, and of Gothic earnestness, with praise of the misjudged pleasures of a young body and a free mind, could supply the humanist with a sufficient inspiration so long as Christian orthodoxy remained dominant; but when the strongholds of superstition and morose tyranny (as he called them) were in ruins, and tenanted only by a few owls or a bevy of cooing pigeons, his angry occupation was gone. The great courts and the great court preachers were humanistic enough. Nothing therefore remained for him but to turn wit, or savant, or polite poet, and to spread his philanthropic sympathies thinner and thinner over all human things. Eastern civilizations claimed a place in his affections side by side with the ancients: he must make room even for savage arts and savage virtues—they were so human—nor could he exclude for ever that wonderful medieval art and philosophy which, in the flush of the Renaissance, he had derided and deposed. Thus humanism ended at last in a pensive agnosticism and a charmed culture, as in the person of Matthew Arnold.

It is against this natural consequence of the old humanism that the new American humanists, in a great measure, seem to be protesting. They feel the lameness of that conclusion: and indeed a universal culture always tolerant, always fluid, smiling on everything exotic and on everything new, sins against the principle of life itself. We exist by distinction, by integration round a specific nucleus according to a particular pattern. Life demands a great insensibility, as well as a great sensibility. If the humanist could really live up to his ancient maxim, *humani nil a me alienum puto,* he would sink into moral anarchy and artistic impotence—the very things from which our liberal, romantic world is so greatly suffering. The three R's of modern history, the Renaissance, the Reformation, and the Revolution, have left the public mind without any vestige of discipline. The old humanism itself is impotent and scattered; no man of the world any longer remembers his Latin.

Indeed, those three R's were inwardly at war with one another. The Renaissance, if it had had full swing, would never have become, even locally or by mistake, either Protestant or revolutionary: what can a pure poet or humanist have in common with religious faction, or with a sentimental faith in liberty and democracy? Such a free mind might really have understood the ancients, and might have passed grandly with them into a complete naturalism, universal and impartial on its intellectual side (since the intellect is by right all-seeing) but in politics and morals fiercely determinate, with an animal and patriotic intensity of will; like Carthage and Sparta, and like the Soviets and the Fascists of today. Such political naturalism was clearly conceived by Bacon and Machiavelli, and by many princes and nobles who took the Protestant side, not in the least for religious reasons, but because they were supermen wishing to be free from all trammels, with a clergy to serve them and all wealth and initiative in their own hands. Those princes and nobles had their day, but the same motives work to this hour in the nations or classes that have taken their place.

I think that in each of the three R's we may distinguish an efficacious hidden current of change in the unconscious world from the veneer of words and sentiments that may have served to justify that change, or to mask it in the popular mind, and often in the mind of the leaders. The Renaissance really tended to emancipate the passions and to exploit nature for fanciful and for practical human uses; it simply continued all that was vivacious and ornate in the Middle Ages. It called those ages barbarous, partly for writing dog Latin and partly for being hard, penitential, warlike, and migratory; one might almost say, for being religious. The mind of the Renaissance was not a pilgrim mind, but a sedentary city mind, like that of the ancients;

in this respect and in its general positivism, the Renaissance was truly a revival of antiquity. If merchants and prince-lings traveled or fought, it was in order to enrich themselves at home, and not because of an inward unrest or an unreturn-ing mission, such as life itself is for a pure soul. If here or there some explorer by vocation or some great philosopher had still existed (and I know of none) he would have been a continuator of the crusaders or the scholastics. A genius typical of the Renaissance, such as Leonardo or Shakespeare, could not be of that consecrated kind. In his omnivorous intelligence and zest, in his multiform contacts and observa-tions, in so many lights kindled inconclusively, such a ge-nius, except for the intensity of his apprehension, would not have been a master or a poet at all. He would have been, like Bacon and Machiavelli, a prophet of Big Business. There might still be passion and richness in the accents, but the tidings were mean. The Renaissance, for all its po-etry, scholarship, and splendor, was a great surrender of the spirit to the flesh, of the essence for the miscellany of human power.

The Reformation in like manner had a mental façade which completely hid the forces that really moved it, and the di-rection in which its permanent achievements would lie. It gave out that it was a religious reform and revival, and it easily enlisted all the shocked consciences, restless intel-lects, and fanatical hearts of the day in its cause; but in its very sincerity it substituted religious experience for reli-gious tradition, and that, if the goal had been really religious, would have been suicide; for in religious experience, taken as its own criterion, there is nothing to distinguish religion from moral sentiment or from sheer madness. Kant and other German philosophers have actually reduced religion to false postulates or dramatic metaphors necessary to the heroic practice of morality. But why practise folly heroically and call it duty? Because conscience bids. And why does conscience bid that? *Because society and empire require it.*

Meantime, in popular quarters, we see religion, or the last shreds of it, identified with occult science or sympathetic medicine. The fact is, I think, that the Reformation from the beginning lived on impatience of religion and appealed to lay interests; to the love of independence, national and personal; to free thought; to local pride; to the lure of plunder and enterprise; to the sanctity of thrift. Many a writer (Macaulay, for instance) demonstrates the superiority of Protestantism by pointing to its social fruits: better roads, neater villages, less begging and cheating, more schools, more commerce, greater scientific advance and philosophic originality. Admirable things, except perhaps the last: and we learn that religion is to be regarded as an instrument for producing a liberal well-being. But when this is secured, and we have creature comforts, a respectable exterior, and complete intellectual liberty, what in turn are the spiritual fruits? None: for the spirit, in this system, is only an instrument, and its function is fulfilled if those earthly advantages are realized. It was so, at bottom, with the ancient Jews: and the intensity of religious emotions in the prophet or the revivalist must not blind us to the tragic materialism at his heart. I think we might say of Protestantism something like what Goethe said of Hamlet. Nature had carelessly dropped an acorn into the ancient vase of religion, and the young oak, growing within, shattered the precious vessel.

In the Revolution (which is not yet finished) the same

doubleness is perhaps less patent: liberty, fraternity, and equality have been actually achieved in some measure, even if they lack that Arcadian purity and nobleness which the revolutionary prophets expected. Their cry had been for limpid virtue, antique heroism, and the radical destruction of unreason: the event has brought industrialism, populousness, comfort, and the dominance of the average man, if not of the average woman.

The whole matter is complicated by the presence of yet another R, Romance, which lies in an entirely different category from the Renaissance, the Reformation, and the Revolution. Romance is not, like these, inspired by any modern sense of outrage or by any moral or political theory. It is neither hortatory nor contemptuous; not a rebellion against anything. I don't know whether its springs should be called Celtic or Norse or simply primitive and human, or whether any subtle currents from Alexandria or Arabia, or from beyond, swelled the flood in the dark ages. Suffice it that Romance is something very old, and supplies that large element which is neither classical nor Christian in medieval and modern feeling. It lies deeper, I think, in most of us than any conventional belief or allegiance. It involves a certain sense of homelessness in a chaotic world, and at the same time a sense of meaning and beauty there. To Romance we owe the spirit of adventure; the code of honor, both masculine and feminine; chivalry and heraldry; feudal loyalty; hereditary nobility; courtesy, politeness, and pity; the love of nature; rhyme and perhaps lyric melody; imaginative love and fidelity; sentimentality; humor. Romance was a great luminous mist blowing from the country into the ancient town; in the wide land of Romance everything was vaguely placed and man migratory; the knight, the troubadour, of the palmer carried all his permanent possessions on his back, or in his bosom. So did the wandering student and the court fool. There was much play with the picturesque and the miraculous; perhaps the cockiness of changing fashions has the same source. Fancy has freer play when men are not deeply respectful to custom or reason, but feel the magic of strangeness and distance, and the profound absurdity of things.

Even the intellect in the romantic world became subject to moods: attention was arrested at the subjective. "Experience"—the story-teller's substance—began to seem more interesting and sure than the causes of experience or the objects of knowledge. The pensive mind learned to trace the Gothic intricacies of music and mathematics, and to sympathize too much with madness any longer to laugh at it. The abnormal might be heroic; and there could be nothing more sure and real than the intense and the immediate. In this direction, Romance developed into British and German philosophy, in which some psychological phantasm, sensuous or logical, interposes itself in front of the physical world, covers and absorbs it. Mixed with revolutionary passions, Romance also produced the philosophy of Rousseau; and mixed with learning and archaeology, the classical revival of Goethe and his time; finally, by a sort of reduplication or reversion of romantic interest upon Romance itself, there followed the literary and architectural romanticism of the nineteenth century.

Romance is evidently a potent ingredient in the ethos of the modern world; and I confess that I can hardly imagine in the near future any poetry, morality, or religion not deeply romantic. Something wistful, a consciousness of imperfec-

tion, the thought of all the other beauties destroyed or renounced in achieving anything, seems inseparable from
breadth in sympathy and knowledge; and such breadth is
the essence of modern enlightenment. But is not this intelligent humility itself a good? Is it not a prerequisite to a sane
happiness? The accident of birth, with all its consequences,
offers us the first and palmary occasion for renunciation,
measure, and reason. Why not frankly rejoice in the benefits,
so new and extraordinary, which our state of society af-
fords? We may not possess those admirable things which
Professor Norton pined for, but at least (besides football)
haven't we Einstein and Freud, Proust and Paul Valéry,
Lenin and Mussolini? For my part, though a lover of antiquity, I should certainly congratulate myself on living
among the moderns, if the moderns were only modern
enough, and dared to face nature with an unprejudiced
mind and a clear purpose. Never before was the mental
landscape so vast. What if the prospect, when the spirit ex-
plores it, seems rather a quagmire, as it were the Marshes of
Glynn, rich only in weak reeds and rank grasses? Has not
the spirit always loved the wilderness? Does not the wide
morass open out here and there into a quiet pool, with
water-lilies, and is not the sky, with all its wonders, often reflected there? Do not the screeching wild-fowl cleave this air
with avidity? I think that the simple lover of the beautiful
may well be content to take his turn and have his day almost anywhere in the pageant of human history. Wherever
he might be born, or wherever banished, he could never be
separated from his inner mind or from a fundamental kin-
ship with his fellow-creatures. Even if his feet were without
foothold in the dreary bog, his spirit need not be starved or
impatient. Amid weeds and rushes, if he would only watch
them, and breathing deep the very freedom of emptiness, he

might forget the oaks and roses of terra firma, even for five hundred or a thousand years.

So far, then, the gist of modern history would seem to be this: a many-sided insurrection of the unregenerate natural man, with all his physical powers and affinities, against the regimen of Christendom. He has convinced himself that his physical life is not as his ghostly mentors asserted, a life of sin; and why should it be a life of misery? Society has gradually become a rather glorious, if troubled, organization of matter, and of man for material achievements. Even our greatest troubles, such as the late war, seem only to accelerate the scientific bridling of matter; troubles do not cease, but surgery and aviation make remarkable progress. Big Business itself is not without its grave worries: wasted production, turbulent labor, rival bosses, and an inherited form of government, by organized parties and elections, which was based on revolutionary maxims, and has become irrelevant to the true work of the modern world if not disastrous for it. Spiritual distress, too, cannot be banished by spiritual anarchy; in obscure privacy and in the sordid tragedies of doubt and of love, it is perhaps more desperate than ever. We live in an age of suicides. Yet this spiritual distress may be disregarded, like bad dreams, so long as it remains isolated and does not organize any industrial revolt or any fresh total discouragement and mystic withdrawal, such as ushered in the triumph of Christianity. For the present, Big Business continues to generate the sort of intelligence and loyalty which it requires; it favors the most startling triumphs of mind in abstract science and mechanical art, without any philosophic commitments regarding their ultimate truth or value.

Indeed, mechanical art and abstract science are other forms

of Big Business, and congruous parts of it. They, too, are
instinctive undertakings, in which ambition, co-öperation,
and rivalry keep the snowball rolling and getting bigger and
bigger. Some day attention will be attracted elsewhere, and
the whole vain thing will melt away unheeded. But while
the game lasts and absorbs all a man's faculties, its rules
become the guides of his life. In the long run, obedience to
them is incompatible with anarchy, even in the single mind.
Either the private anarchy will ruin public order, or the
public order will cure private anarchy.

The latter, on the whole, has happened in the United States,
and may be expected to become more and more characteristic of the nation. There, according to one of the new
humanists, "The accepted vision of a good life is to make a
lot of money by fair means; to spend it generously; to be
friendly; to move fast; to die with one's boots on." This
sturdy ideal has come to prevail naturally, despite the
preachers and professors of sundry finer moralities; it includes virtue and it includes happiness, at least in the
ancient and virile sense of these words. We are invited to
share an industrious, cordial, sporting existence, self-im-
posed and self-rewarding. There is plenty of room, in the
margin and in the pauses of such a life, for the intellectual
tastes which any one may choose to cultivate; people may
associate in doing so; there will be clubs, churches, and
colleges by the thousand; and the adaptable spirit of Protestantism may be relied upon to lend a pious and philosophical sanction to any instinct that may deeply move the
national mind.

Why should any one be dissatisfied? Is it not enough that
millionaires splendidly endow libraries and museums, that
the democracy loves them, and that even the Bolsheviks

prize the relics of Christian civilization when laid out in that funeral documentary form? Is it not enough that the field lies open for any young professor in love with his subject to pursue it hopefully and ecstatically, until perhaps it begins to grow stale, the face of it all cracked and wrinkled with little acrid controversies and perverse problems? And when not pressed so far, is it not enough that the same studies should supply a pleasant postscript to business, a congenial hobby or night-cap for ripe, rich, elderly people? May not the ardent humanist still cry (and not in the wilderness): Let us be well-balanced, let us be cultivated, let us be high-minded; let us control ourselves, as if we were wild; let us chasten ourselves, as if we had passions; let us learn the names and dates of all famous persons; let us travel and see all the pictures that are starred in Baedeker; let us establish still more complete museums at home, and sometimes visit them in order to show them to strangers; let us build still more immense libraries, containing all known books, good, bad, and indifferent, and let us occasionally write reviews of some of them, so that the public, at least by hearsay, may learn which are which.

Why be dissatisfied? I am sure that the true heirs to the three R's would not ask for more. Even Romance gets its due; what could be more romantic than the modern world, like a many-decked towering liner, a triumph of mechanism, a hive of varied activities, sailing for sailing's sake? Big Business is an amiable monster, far kindlier and more innocent than anything Machiavelli could have anticipated, and no less lavish in its patronage of experiment, invention, and finery than Bacon could have desired. The discontent of the American humanists would be unintelligible if they were really humanists in the old sense; if they represented in some measure the soul of that young oak, bursting the limits of Christendom. Can it be that they represent rather the shattered urn, or some one of its fragments? The leaders, indeed, though hardly their followers, might pass for rather censorious minds, designed by nature to be the pillars of some priestly orthodoxy; and their effort, not as yet very successful, seems to be to place their judgments upon a philosophical basis.

After all, we may actually be witnessing the demise of the genteel tradition, though by a death more noble and glorious than some of us had looked for. Instead of expiring of fatigue, or evaporating into a faint odor of learning and sentiment hanging about Big Business, this tradition, in dying, may be mounting again to its divine source. In its origin it was a severe and explicit philosophy, Calvinism; not essentially humanistic at all, but theocratic. Theocracy is what all the enemies of the three R's, and more, the enemies of Romance, must endeavor to restore, if they understand their own position. Wealth, learning, sport, and beneficence, even on a grand scale, must leave them cold, or positively alarm them, if these fine things are not tightly controlled and meted out according to some revealed absolute standard. Culture won't do, they must say, unless it be the one right culture: learning won't do, unless it fills out the one true philosophy. No more sentimentality, then, or intellectual snobbery; away with the sunset glow and the organ peals overheard in a churchyard. Let us have honest bold dogmas supported by definite arguments; let us re-establish our moral sentiments on foundations more solid than tradition or gentility. Boundless liberal opportunity, such as Big Business offers, is a futile romantic lure. Even the most favorable turn of the fashion in education, criticism, and literature would not last for ever. The opposite schools would continue to advertise their wares; and only the unpredictable shifts of human moods and customs could here or there decide the issue. The best fruits of time, in any case, are unexpected. If our edifice is to be safe, we must lay the foundations in eternity.

Is this really the meaning of the American humanists, which they have hardly ventured to propose, even to themselves? If so, the summons is bold and the programme radical: nothing less than to brush away the four R's from the education and the sentiment of the modern world, and to reinstate a settled belief in a supernatural human soul and in a precise divine revelation. These, as they say in Spain, are major words, and we shall have to proceed with caution.

II

The Appeal to the Supernatural

Almost all nations and religions, and especially the liberal party in them, think themselves the salt of the earth. They believe that only their special institutions are normal or just, and hope to see them everywhere adopted. They declare that only the scriptures handed down by their own clergy are divinely inspired; that only their native language is clear, convenient, deeply beautiful, and ultimately destined to become universal; that only the logic of their home philosophers is essentially cogent; and that the universal rule of morals, if not contained in tablets preserved in their temple, is concentrated in an insoluble pellet of moral prejudice, like the categorical imperative of Kant, lodged in their breast. Not being content, or not being able, to cultivate their local virtues in peace at home, they fiercely desire to sweep everything foreign from the face of the earth. Is this madness? No: I should say it was only haste, transposing a vital necessity into absurd metaphysical terms. Moral absolutism is the shadow of moral integrity.

Now moral integrity and its shadow, moral absolutism, were always a chief part of the genteel tradition in America. They were perhaps its essence; and we need not wonder that the heirs to this tradition, in order to reaffirm the integrity of soul which they feel to be slipping away from them, clutch at its shadow, ethical absolutism, which perhaps they think is its principle. But such principles are verbal; they are not sources; and absolutism, even if reinstated philosophically, would never actually re-establish integrity in a dissolute mind or in a chaotic society. The natural order of derivation and growth is the opposite, and nature must first produce a somewhat integrated soul before that soul can discover or pursue the ideal of integrity.

Nevertheless, merely to reinstate absolutism philosophically would be a great feat, and would prove the hopeless perversity of relaxing integrity in any degree whatever. If, for instance, the human soul were supernatural and had its proper life and perfection in another world, then indeed all the variety of human tastes, temperaments, and customs would be variety only in self-ignorance and error. There would be an external criterion, apart from all places, persons, and times, by which everything should be judged, namely: Does this conduce to the salvation of the soul? Salvation would mean self-recovery, emergence from distraction, life beginning anew, not romantically, in some arbitrary fresh adventure in an exotic landscape, but inwardly, by the pure exercise of those functions which are truly native and sufficent to the spirit. The supernatural constitution and affinities of the soul would supply a criterion for all human affairs; not one absurdly imposed by one earthly creature upon another, as I was just now protesting, but one imposed by the visiting spirit upon the whole natural world. For however admirable and innocent the whole life of nature might be in itself, it would probably be in some directions sympathetic and in others poisonous and horrible to the native of a different sphere.

What, then, would a supernatural world be if it existed? I don't mean to ask what such a world would contain: it might evidently contain anything. I am only asking what relation any occult world must bear to nature, as we know nature, if that other world is to deserve the titles of existent and of supernatural. If it is to be existent, and not like the realms of poetry or mathematics merely conceived, it must, I think, be in dynamic relations with ourselves and with our world. Miracles, reports, incarnations, and ascensions, or at least migrations of the soul, must connect the two worlds, and make them, in reality, parts of one and the same universe. The supramundane and the mundane taken together would compose the total reality with which human knowledge, morality, and sentiment must reckon if they would not be ultimately stultified by the facts.

Supernaturalism, in its own eyes, is accordingly simply a completed naturalism, a naturalism into which certain ulterior facts and forces, hidden from our near-sighted and imperfect science, have been duly admitted. The morality inspired by supernaturalism will also be a naturalistic morality in principle: only that the soul will then be confronted by other opportunities and other dangers than her earthly life contains. Reason will have to take longer views, and the passions will be arrested, excited, or transformed by a larger prospect.

On the other hand, if this possible other world is to be called supernatural in any significant sense, it must not be confused with the chaotic, the groundlessly miraculous, the *infra*-natural. I am far from wishing to deny that the infra-natural exists; that below the superficial order which our senses and science find in the world, or impose upon it, there may not be an intractable region of incalculable accidents, chance novelties, or inexplicable collapses. Perhaps what we call the order of nature may be only a cuticle imperfectly formed round a liquid chaos. This speculative possibility is worth entertaining in the interests of scientific modesty and spiritual detachment; and it positively fascinates some ultra-romantic minds, that detest to be caged even in an infinite world, if there is any order in it. Indetermination seems to them liberty; they feel that idiocy and accident are far more deeply rooted than method in their own being, and they think it must be so also in the world at large: and perhaps they are right. All this underlying chaos, however, if it exists, has nothing to do with that supernatural sphere—a sphere and not medley—to which morality and religion may be tempted to appeal. As the Indian, Platonic, and Christian imagination has conceived it, the supernatural has an external nature and a sublime order of its own. It forms an elder cosmos surrounding our nether world and destined to survive it. In that cosmos a hierarchy of spirits continually descends and ascends all the steps of moral decline and exaltation; and there the inexplicable burdens and tantalizing glories of this life find their origin and their fulfillment.

There is nothing impossible, therefore, in the existence of the supernatural: its existence seems to me decidedly probable; there is infinite room for it on every side. But, then, this almost tangible supernatural world is only the rest of nature, nature in her true depths and in her true infinity, which is presumably a rich and unmapped infinity of actual being, not the cheap ideal infinity of the geometers. The question is only what evidences we may have of the existence of this hidden reality, and of its character; whether, for instance, it is likely that the outlying parts of the universe should be more sympathetic to our moral nature than this particular part to which we are native, and which our science describes, because this is the part which we have to reckon with in action.

Now to this question the Platonic and Christian tradition replies, among other things, that the soul herself is a sufficient witness to her own supernatural origin, faculties, and destiny, inasmuch as she knows herself to be a pure spirit, synthetic and intelligent, endowed with free will, and immortal. We are not really native to this world, except in respect to our bodies; our souls are native to a spiritual world, from which we fetch our standards of truth and beauty, and in which alone we can be happy. Such is the thesis: and we must never let this ancient citadel of absolutism fall into the enemy's hands if we expect safely to hold the outworks and to claim for ourselves a universal jurisdiction in taste, politics, and morals. Moreover, this citadel encloses a sanctuary: our philosophical supernaturalism would be uselessly vague without a positive revelation.

If we were not especially informed concerning the nature and destiny of all human souls, how could we legislate for them universally? How could we assert that all types of virtue, except our one official type, are either rudimentary or corrupt, and that although biologically various types radiate from a centre and diverge more and more the nearer they come to perfection, morally this is not so, but all human souls, in spite of what they may think, can be saved only by marching compulsorily in single file, after the same kind of happiness? We must possess a divine revelation to this effect, since without such a revelation our moral dogmatism would be avowedly only an expression of our particular temperament or local customs; and any romantic anarchist or dissolute epicurean might flout us, saying that his temperament and his customs were as good as our own or, to his feeling, better; and that he was innocent and happy in his way of life, and at peace with God— as indeed that loose, low creature, Walt Whitman, actually declared.

And the case would be particularly hopeless if the heretics, like us, were supernaturalists about the soul; because if they were mere naturalists we might rebuke them on medical grounds, as we warn a child munching too many sweets of the stomach-ache and the toothache, lest he should be cloyed too late; or we might simply turn the cold shoulder of indifference and disgust upon the odious being, to signify his ostracism from our desirable society. But if he too was an immortal visitor from another world, he might well despise our earthly prudence and stupid persecutions, and he might assert against us his own unassailable vocation merely to will, or merely to laugh, or merely to understand. How, unless divinely illuminated, could we then pretend that we knew what was good for him better than he knew it himself? Nothing would be left for us except to thrash him: which at present we should be wisely disinclined to attempt; because in the arena of democratic jealousies and journalistic eloquence he would probably thrash us. No; we must boldly threaten him with hell fire; he shall be thrashed in the other world, in the world of spirit to which he appeals; and though the more picturesque forms of this threat may be out of date, and may raise a smile, there are other forms of it terrible enough in themselves and near to our daily experience. We have but to open the newspaper to read the last confidences of some suicide, and to learn how the torments and the darkness of hell descend on the desperate rebel and the forlorn pleasure seeker. We must rely on the horror which the facts of earthly life, when faced, inspire in the innocent conscience. We must appeal to the profound doubt, the profound unhappiness, the profound courage in the human soul, so that she may accept our revelation as the key to the mystery of her profound ignorance.

The alleged happiness of the epicurean or the romantic we must assert to be a lie. In them, too, we must believe, a supernatural Christian soul is leading a painful and disgusted life; for nothing can be more unnatural to her than naturalism. Evil souls and ugly bodies are degenerate, not primitive; we are all wretchedly fallen from an estate to which we secretly aspire to return, although we may not clearly perceive our plight or understand the nature of that good which alone would render us happy. We need to have the way of salvation preached to us, whether it be salvation in this world or in another; and this preaching we must receive on authority, if not on that of a special religion, at least that of the high philosophic tradition, Indian, Neo-platonic, and Catholic, which represents the spiritual wisdom of all ages. If we reject this authority and neglect to seek the supernatural happiness which it prescribes, we shall be systematically sinning against ourselves, and literally losing our souls.

The same doctrine of a supernatural soul is indispensable if we would justify another conviction dear to the absolute moralist; I mean, the consciousness of free will. A supernatural soul would have a life and direction of her own: she would be an efficacious member of an invisible cosmos, in which—since the whole is the work of God—every being would have its appropriate gifts, functions, and destiny. The soul cannot create herself: she cannot determine the point of space and time at which she will begin to show her colors: she cannot tell how long her influence may be allowed to count in this world. But while her union with the body endures, there will be a tug-of-war; and the issue will never be determined by either side taken alone. A man will therefore be no helpless slave of his body; his acts will not be predetermined physically without his soul's leave; they will be determined by the interplay of the physical with the spiritual forces in him: and on the spiritual side there will be two principal factors; his soul, with her native powers, affinities, and will, and the will and the grace of God, putting that soul in contact with particular circumstances and allowing her in that trial some measure of victory.

The soul, being an independent centre of force, would have come, on this hypothesis, into the body from without, and would continue to act upon it from within, until perhaps she escaped to pursue elsewhere her separate fortunes. This independent initiative of hers would be her free will: free in respect to material laws or solicitations, but of course conformable to her own instinct and native direction, as well as subject to the original dispositions and dynamic balance of the total universe, natural and supernatural. We must not confuse the dualism of origin in human acts, asserted by this theory of a supernatural soul, with any supposed absolute indetermination of either soul or body, or of their natural effects upon one another. Indeterminism, if it exists, belongs to the unintelligible foundations of things, to chaos, and to the sub-human: it is so far from vindicating the power of spirit over matter, that in this contest, as everywhere else, a real indeterminism would dislocate the normal relations of things and render them, to that extent, fortuitous.

The notion that absolute freedom might save many a critical situation, and that in general the intervention of groundless movements would tend towards a happy issue rests on a complete confusion. It is the gambler's fallacy. Empty possibility seems to him full of promise; but in fact sheer chance, throwing dice, would seldom throw sixes. The only force that really tends towards happy results is the innate force of the soul herself: for the soul, whether natural or supernatural, is an organizing principle working, as in seeds, for a particular form of life which, if realized, would make her good and her perfection. If in this labor any groundless events occurred in her or in the circumstances, she would to that extent be the victim of chance. Energies dropped into her and not exerted by herself would evidently do no work of hers; they would not manifest her freedom, but only her helplessness; they would be irruptions into her life of that primitive contingency which is identical with fate. The result would, to that extent, not be after her own mind, and she would not be responsible for it. Sheer indeterminism like the danger of earthquakes, if the healthy mind did not disregard it, would put all human labor in jeopardy: it would dislocate all definite hopes and calculations; in a sane life it would be the worst and the most alien of agencies. Such a possibility is like the other face of the moon, for ever turned away from human interests.

The kind of free will which concerns the moralist asserts rather the autonomy of the soul, her power of manifesting herself, often surprisingly, in the realm of matter in ways which, since they express her innate impulses, may have been already vaguely prefigured and desired by her conscious mind. This freedom, or external initiative, will be proper to the soul whether she be natural or supernatural: in either case she will have a chosen good to pursue, and a certain limited power of achieving it; but if she is natural, her dispositions may change with the evolution of animal life, and one of her forms will have no authority over another; whereas, if she is supernatural, these material shifts will change only the theatre of her activity or its instruments; her nature and her perfection will remain unchangeable.

If, then, the American humanists hope to maintain an absolute criterion of taste and morals, I think they should hasten to embrace supernaturalism, in case they have not done so already. The word supernatural has long been out of favor, partly because it denied to science an omniscience which, in theory, science never claimed, and partly be-

cause it pointed to possible realities far beyond that subjective sphere which is the only reality admitted by romantic
idealism: but neither reason seems to have any serious
force. Supernaturalism, being an extension of naturalism, is
far sounder philosophically than subjectivism, and morally
at once humbler and more sublime. And that form of
supernaturalism which lies nearest at hand, Christian Platonism, has the further advantage, in this case, of being
remarkably humanistic. It deifies human morality and human intelligence.

Socrates and Plato, and some of the Fathers of the Church,
were excellent humanists. They had not, of course, that
great rhetorical joy in all the passions which we find in
the humanists of the Renaissance and, somewhat chastened,
in Shakespeare. Platonism and Christianity, in their beginnings, were reactions against decadence, and necessarily
somewhat disillusioned and ascetic. These philosophers
were absorbed in preaching: I mean, in denouncing one-
half of life and glorifying the other half; they were absolute moralists; and this dominance of ethical interests was
confirmed by the Jewish and the Roman influences which
permeated that age. Moreover a learned humanism was involved in the possession of Scriptures, demanding studies
and eloquent expositions, which could not remain exclusively theological or legendary. In the Old Testament and
even in the New, there were humanistic maxims, such as
that the Sabbath was made for man, and not man for the
Sabbath. Epicurus had crept into Ecclesiastes, and Plato
into the Gospel of Saint John; and by a bolder stroke of
humanism than any one had yet thought of, God himself
had been made man. Man consequently might be super-
latively important in his own eyes, without offence to the

higher powers. He might proclaim his natural preferences even more vehemently and tenaciously than the heathen since round his conscience and his intellect he believed that the universe revolved, and had indeed been created expressly for his dubious and tragic glory.

This marked, and even absolute, humanism in Platonism and Christianity seems indeed to some of us, who have no prejudice against supernaturalism in general, an argument against supernaturalism of that kind. There is a sort of acoustic illusion in it: the voice that reverberates from the heavens is too clearly a human voice. Is it not obvious that the reports contained in this revelation are not bits of sober information, not genuine reminiscences of a previous life, not messages literally conveyed from other worlds by translated prophets or visiting angels? Are they not clearly human postulates, made by ignorant mortals in sheer desperation or in poetic self-indulgence? Are they not ways of imagining a material vindication of lost causes, by a miraculous reversal, in the last instance, of every judgment of fate? Don Quixote, after twice mending and testing his ancestral helmet, and finding it fall apart at the first blow, mended it for the third time with a green riband—green being the color of hope—and, without testing it this time, deputed it to be henceforth a trusty and a perfect helmet. So when native zeal and integrity, either in nations or in persons, has given way to fatigue or contagion, a supernatural assurance needing no test may take possession of the mind. Plato wrote his "Republic" after Athens had succumbed, and his "Laws" after Syracuse had disappointed him; Neo-platonism and Christianity became persuasive when ancient civic life had lost its savor. A wealth of wisdom survived, but little manly courage; a dreamful courage of another sort, supernatural faith, transposed that wisdom into meekness; and sanctity sprouted like the early crocus in the loam under the leafless giants of antiquity.

Far be it from me to suggest that anybody ought to exchange his native religion or morality for a foreign one: he would be merely blighting in himself the only life that was really possible. But the travelling thoughts of the pure philosopher may compare the minds and manners of various men; and considering the supernatural world of Platonism and Christianity, he may marvel to observe how very mundane that supernatural world is, how moralistic and romantic, how royal, ecclesiastical, legal, and dramatic an apotheosis of national or pious ambitions. At best, as in Plotinus, it lifts to cosmic dimensions the story of spiritual experience. But how shall any detached philosopher believe that the whole universe, which may be infinite, is nothing but an enlarged edition, or an expurgated edition, of human life? This is only a daylight religion; the heavens in its view are near, and pleasantly habitable by the Olympians; the spheres fit the earth like a glove; the sky is a tent spread protectingly or shaken punitively over the human nest.

In the East, the philosopher will remember, there are, as it were, night religions, simpler perhaps than ours but more metaphysical, inspired by the stars or the full moon. Taken as information, their account of the other world is no better than ours, but their imagination is more disinterested and their ontology bolder. They are less afraid that the truth might be disconcerting. Is the color which those inhuman religions lend to morality less suitable to mankind? I am sure that a Hindu, a Moslem, or a Buddhist is amply sustained in his home virtues by his traditional precepts and rites; he does not need to transpose these virtues out of their human sphere; the universe can sanction in man the virtues proper to man without needing to imitate them on its own immeasurable scale.

That was a confused and insolent ambition in Milton to justify the ways of God to man. Impartial reflection upon ultimate things tends to purify, without condemning, all the natural passions, because being natural, they are inevitable and inherently innocent, while being *only* natural, they are all relative and, in a sense, vain. Platonism and Christianity, on the contrary, except in a few natural mystics and speculative saints, seem to sacrifice ruthlessly one set of passions merely in order to intensify another set. Ultimate insights cannot change human nature; but they may remove that obfuscation which accompanies any passion, and a virtuous passion especially, when its relativity is not understood. Human nature includes intelligence, and cannot therefore be perfected without such an illumination, and the equipoise which it brings: and this would seem to be a better fruit of meditation upon the supernatural than any particular regimen to be forced upon mankind in the name of heaven. Not that the particular regimen sanctified by Platonic and Christian moralists is at all inacceptable; but they did not require any supernatural assistance to draw it up. They simply received back from revelation the humanism which they had put into it.

III

The Moral Adequacy of Naturalism

Suppose we discount as fabulous every projection of human morality into the supernatural: need we thereby relapse into moral anarchy? In one sense, and from the point of view of the absolute or monocular moralist, we must; because the whole moral sphere then relapses into the bosom of nature, and nature, though not anarchical, is not governed by morality. But for a philosopher with two eyes, the natural status of morality in the animal world does not exclude the greatest vigor in those moral judgments and moral passions which belong to his nature. On the contrary, I think that it is only when he can see the natural origin and limits of the moral sphere that a moralist can be morally sane and just. Blindness to the biological truth about morality is not favorable to purity of moral feeling: it removes all sense of proportion and relativity; it kills charity, humility, and humor; and it shuts the door against that ultimate light which comes to the spirit from the spheres above morality.

The Greeks—if I may speak like Professor Norton—the early Greeks, who as yet had little experience of philosophers, sometimes invited their philosophers to legislate for them. Their problem was not so unlike that which confronts us today: in the midst of increasing bustle and numbers, the preponderance of towns, the conflict of classes, close and dangerous foreign relations, freer manners, new ideas in science and art. How did those early sages set to work? In one way, they didn't mince matters: the rule of life which each of them proposed for his city covered the whole life of the citizen, military, political, intellectual, ceremonial, and athletic: but on the other hand, for each city the rule proposed was different: severe and unchangeable at Sparta, liberal and variable at Athens; while the idealistic brotherhood of the Pythagoreans prescribed astronomy and sweet numbers for Magna Graecia. It was in quite other circumstances that Socrates and Plato,

Moses and President Wilson came forward to legislate un-asked, and for the universe.

I am afraid that even some of those earlier sages were not perfect naturalists. They did not merely consider the ex-tant organism for which they were asked to prescribe, or endeavor to disentangle, in its own interests, the diseases or dangers which might beset it. A legislating naturalist would be like a physican or horticulturalist or breeder of animals: he would remove obstructions and cut out barren deformities; he would have a keen eye for those variations which are spontaneous and fertile, gladly giving them free play; and he would know by experience those other vari-ations into which nature may be coaxed by grafting and watering. In all his measures he would be guided by the avowed needs and budding potentialities of his client. Perhaps some of those Greek law-givers, the Pythagoreans, for instance, had something of the missionary about them, and while full of adoration for the harmonies of nature as they conceived them, conceived these harmonies idealis-tically, and felt called upon to correct nature by the au-thority of a private oracle. In this their philosophy, apart from some cosmological errors, may have proved its depth, and may have been prophetic of the revolution that was destined to undermine ancient society.

The only natural unit in morals is the individual man, be-cause no other natural unit is synthesized by nature herself into a living spirit. The state is only a necessary cradle for the body of the individual, and nursery for his mind; and he can never really renounce his prescriptive right to shatter the state or to reform it, according to his physical and spiritual necessities. Even when his spontaneous fidelity causes him to forget or to deny this right, the force of fidelity is at that very moment exercising that right within him. Yet it was an intermediate and somewhat artificial unit, the ancient city, that was asking those early philosophers for counsel; and that counsel could not be good, or honestly given, unless it considered the life of the individual within the walls, and the life of the world outside, only as they might contribute to the perfection of the city.

Morality—by which I mean the principle of all choices in taste, faith, and allegiance—has a simple natural ground. The living organism is not infinitely elastic; if you stretch it too much, it will snap; and it justifiably cries out against you somewhat before the limit is reached. This animal obstinacy is the backbone of all virtue, though intelligence, convention, and sympathy may very much extend and soften its expression. As the brute unconditionally wills to live, so the man, especially the strong masterful man, unconditionally wills to live after a certain fashion. To be pliant, to be indefinite, seems to him ignominious.

Very likely, in his horror of dissipating his strength or deviating from his purpose, he will give opprobrious names to every opposite quality. His hot mind may not be able to conceive as virtues in others any traits which would not be virtues in himself. Yet this moral egotism, though common or even usual, is not universal in virtuous people. On the contrary, precisely those who are most perfect escape it: they do not need the support of the majority, or of the universal voice, in order to fortify them in some shaky allegiance. They know what they want and what they love: the evident beauty of the beautiful is not enhanced or removed by agreement. In its victorious actuality a man's work must be local and temporary: it satisfies his impulse in his day, and he is not forbidden to feel that in some secret sense the glory of it is eternal. In this way aristocratic people, who are sure of their own taste and manners, are indifferent, except for a general curiosity, to the disputes of critics and pedants, and perhaps to the maxims of preachers; such things are imposing only to those who are inwardly wondering what they ought to do, and how they ought to feel. A truly enlightened mind is all the simpler for being enlightened and thinks, not without a modest sort of irony, that art and life exist to be enjoyed and not to be estimated. Why should different estimations annoy any one who is not a snob, when, if they are sincere, they express different enjoyments?

Accordingly, a reasonable physican of the soul would leave his patients to prescribe for themselves, though not before subjecting them to a Socratic or even Freudian inquisition, or searching of heart, in order to awaken in them a radical self-knowledge, such as amid conventions and verbal illusions they probably do not possess. Evidently a regimen determined in this way has no validity for any other being, save in the measure in which, as a matter of fact, that other being partakes in the same nature and would find his sincere happiness in the same things. This is seldom or never exactly the case. Nothing is more multiform than perfection. No interest, no harmony, shuts out the legitimacy or the beauty of any other. It only shuts out from itself those qualities which are incompatible with perfection of that kind, there: as the perfect diamond shuts out the ruby, and the perfect ruby rejects the lovely color of the emerald. But from nature, in her indefinite plasticity, nothing is shut out *a priori;* and no sort of virtue need be excluded by a rational moralist from the place where that virtue is native, and may be perfect.

Perfection is the most natural form of existence, simply carrying out the organic impulse by which any living creature arises at all; nor can that impulse ever find its quietus and satisfaction short of perfection; and nevertheless perfection is rare and seems wonderful, because division or weakness within the organism, or contrariety without, usually nips perfection in the bud. These biological troubles have their echo in the conscience. The alternation between pride and cowardice, between lust and shame, becomes a horrible torment to the spirit; and the issue in any case is unhappy, because a divided soul cannot be perfected. This distress, grown permanent, probably infects the imagination. Mysterious half-external forces—demons and duties— are seen looming behind these contrary natural promptings; and fantastic sanctions, heaven and hell, are invented for the future, enormously exaggerating the terrors of the choice. Thus while on the whole morality which men impose on themselves is rational, the reasons which they give for it are apt to be insane.

What is reason? There is a certain plasticity in some organisms which enables them to profit by experience. Instead of pushing for ever against a stone wall, they learn to go round it or over it. This plasticity, even when not under pressure, may take to play and experiment; toys are made which may become instruments; and the use of sounds as signals may enable the talking animal to recall absent things and to anticipate the future. Moreover, many animals mimic what they see; they transpose themselves dramatically into the objects surrounding them, especially into other animals of the same species. This transposition gives a moral reality, in their own spirit, to all their instinctive coaxing, deceiving, or threatening of one another. Their mind begins to conceive and to compare mere possibilities; it turns to story-telling and games; life becomes a tangle of eager plans and ambitions; and in quiet moments the order of merely imaginary things grows interesting for its own sake. There is a pleasure in embracing several ideas in a single act of intuition so as to see how far they are identical or akin or irrelevant.

Such a power of intellectual synthesis is evidently the mental counterpart of the power of acting with reference to changing or eventual circumstances: whether in practice or in speculation, it is the faculty of putting two and two together, and this faculty is what we call reason. It is what the idiot lacks, the fool neglects, and the madman contradicts. But in no case is reason a code, an oracle, or an external censor condemning the perceptions of sense or suppressing animal impulses. On the contrary, in the moral life, reason is a harmony of the passions, a harmony which perceptions and impulses may compose in so far as they grow sensitive to one another, and begin to move with mutual deference and a total grace.

Such at least was the life of reason which the humanists of the Renaissance thought they discovered, as it were embalmed, in Greek philosophy, poetry, and sculpture. Socrates had expressed this principle paradoxically when he taught that virtue is knowledge—self-knowledge taken to heart and applied prudently in action. Not that spontaneous preferences, character, and will could be dispensed with: these were presupposed; but it was reason that alone could mold those animal components of human nature into a noble and modest happiness.

But is there anything compulsory in reason? Is there not still liberty for fools? Can reason reasonably forbid them to exist? Certainly not, if they like to be fools: I should be sorry to see reason so uselessly kicking against the pricks. But a naturally synthetic mind (and all mind is naturally synthetic) hates waste and confusion; it hates action and speech at cross purposes; and these instinctive aversions implicitly pledge all mind to the ideal of a perfect rationality. Nobody is forbidden to be mindless; but in the mindful person the passions have spontaneously acquired a sense of responsibility to one another; or if they still allow themselves to make merry separately—because liveliness in the parts is a good without which the whole would be lifeless—yet the whole possesses, or aspires to possess, a unity of direction, in which all the parts may conspire, even if unwittingly.

So far, reason might be said to be prescriptive, and to impose a method on all moral life. Yet even where this method is exemplified in action, and life has become to that extent rational, nothing is prescribed concerning the elements which shall enter into that harmony. The materials for the synthesis are such at each point as nature and accident have made them; even in the same man or in the same nation they will be shifting perpetually, so that equally rational beings may have utterly disconnected interests, or interests hopelessly opposed. This diversity will be acceptable, so long as the parties are isolated, like China before the age of discoverers and missionaries; but where there is physical contact and contagion, the appeal must be to war, or to some other form of continued material pressure, such as industrial development or compulsory education: and in such a conflict both sides are apt to lose their original virtues, while the unthought-of virtues of the compound arise in their place.

In another direction the criterion of reason leaves the texture of life undetermined: the degree of unison requisite for harmony may differ in different rational systems. It is perhaps a classical prejudice that all happiness should be architectural. It might be simple and, like disillusioned Christian charity, alms for the moment. The finality of the incidental is more certain, and may be no less perfect, than the finality of great totals, like a life or a civilization. A good verse is much more unmistakably good than a good epic. Organization is everywhere presupposed, otherwise there could be no bodily life and no moral intuition: but where the level of intuition is reached, which is the supreme or spiritual level, the dead mass of the pyramid beneath that apex becomes indifferent. Reason cannot prescribe the girth of a man, or his stature; it can only reveal to his imperfect self his possible perfection. On this account I am not sure that the romantic temperament or art can be condemned off-hand for not being organic enough. Why be so pervasively organic? A flood of details and an alteration of humors may possibly bring the human heart as near as it can come to the heart of things, which I suspect is very fluid; and perhaps the human spirit is not at its best in the spider-like task of construction. Contemplation is freer and may be contemplation of anything.

Why is naturalism supposed to be favorable to the lower sides of human nature? Are not the higher sides just as natural? If anything, the naturalist, being a philosopher, might be expected to move most congenially and habitually on the higher levels. Perhaps the prejudice comes from the accident that when one element of human nature is reinforced by a supernatural sanction, and falsely assigned to a specially divine influence, the unsanctioned remainder alone retains the name of the natural. So Zola can come to be regarded as more naturalistic than Shakespeare, because more sordid in his naturalism, and less adequate; and Shakespeare can be regarded as more naturalistic than Virgil, although Virgil's feeling for things rural as well as for the cosmos at large was more naturalistic than Shakespeare's. Virgil is less romantic, playful, and vague: for the ancients poetized the actual surroundings and destiny of man, rather than the travesty of these facts in human fancy, and the consequent dramas within the spirit.

I think that pure reason in the naturalist may attain, without subterfuge, all the spiritual insights which supernaturalism goes so far out of the way to inspire. Spirituality is only a sort of return to innocence, birdlike and childlike. Experience of the world may have complicated the picture without clouding the vision. In looking before and after, and learning to take another man's point of view, ordinary intelligence has already transcended a brutal animality; it has learned to conceive things as they are, disinterestedly, contemplatively. Although intellect arises quite naturally, in the animal act of dominating events in the interests of survival, yet essentially intellect disengages itself from that servile office (which is that of its organ only) and from the beginning is speculative and impartial in its own outlook, and thinks it not robbery to take the point of view of God, of the truth, and of eternity.

In this congenital spiritual life of his, man regards himself as one creature among a thousand others deserving to be subordinated and kept in its place in his own estimation: a spiritual life not all at war with animal interests, which it presupposes, but detached from them in allegiance, withdrawn into the absolute, and reverting to them only with a charitable and qualified sympathy, such as the sane man can have for the madman, or the soul in general for inanimate things: and of course, it is not only others that the spiritual man regards in this way, but primarily himself. Yet this gift of transcending humanity in sympathy with the truth is a part, and the most distinctive part, of human nature. Reason vindicates insights and judgments which, though overruling those of the world, overrule them within the human heart, with its full consent and to its profound peace and satisfaction. The disillusioned philosopher is (at least in his own opinion) happier than the fool: the saint is at least as human as the man in the street, and far more steadfast and unrepining in his type of humanity.

That the fruition of happiness is intellectual (or as perhaps we should now call it, aesthetic) follows from the comprehensive scope of that intuition in which happiness is realized, a scope which distinguishes happiness from carnal pleasures; for although happiness, like everything else, can be experienced only in particular moments, it is found in conceiving the total issue and ultimate fruits of life; and no passing sensation or emotion could be enjoyed with a free mind, unless the blessing of reason and of a sustained happiness were felt to hang over it. All experience can of course never by synthesized in act, because life is a passage and has many centres; yet such a synthesis is adumbrated everywhere; and when it is partially attained, in some reflective or far-seeing moment, it raises the mind to a contemplation which is very far from cold, being in fact ecstatic; yet this ecstasy remains intellectual in that it holds together the burden of many successive and disparate things, which in blind experience would exclude one another: somewhat as a retentive ear, in a silence following upon music, may gather up the mounting strains of it in a quiet rapture. In raising truth to intuition of truth, in surveying the forms and places of many things at once and conceiving their movement, the intellect performs the most vital of possible acts, locks flying existence, as if were, in its arms, and stands, all eyes and breathless, at the top of life.

Reason may thus lend itself to sublimation into a sort of virtual omniscience or divine ecstasy: yet even then reason remains a harmony of material functions spiritually realized, as in Aristotle the life of God realizes spiritually the harmonious revolutions of the heavens. So it is with reason in morals. It is essential to the validity of a moral maxim that it should be framed in the interest of natural impulses: otherwise that maxim would be a whim or an impertinence. The human impulses to be harmonized should not be without a certain persistence and strength; they should be honest, self-renewing, and self-rewarding, so as not to prove treacherous factors in the method of life to be adopted; and this method in its turn, becoming a custom and an institution, should be a gracious thing, beautiful and naturally glorious, as are love, patriotism, and religion; else the passion for living in political and religious union, beyond the limits of utility, would be sheer folly. But there are fusions, transmutations, and self-surrenders in which a naturally social animal finds an ultimate joy. True reason restrains only to liberate; it checks only in order that all currents, mingling in that moment's pause, may take a united course.

As to conscience and the sense of imposed duty, we may suppose them to be the voice of reason conveyed by tradition, in words that have grown mysterious and archaic, and at the same time solemn and loud. In so far as conscience is not this, but really a personal and groundless sentiment, it may be left to cancel its own oracles. Those who have lived in Boston—and who else should know?—are aware how earnestly the reformed New England conscience now disapproves of its disapprovals. Positive blushes and an awkward silence fall on a worthy family of my acquaintance at the least mention of one of their ancestors, who once wrote a terrifying poem about the Day of Doom. Conscience is an index to integrity of character, and under varying circumstances may retain an iron rigidity, like the staff and arrow of a weather-vane; but if directed by sentiment only, and not by a solid science of human nature, conscience will always be pointing in a different direction.

And in what direction exactly, we may ask, does conscience point so impressively in the American humanists, that they feel constrained to invoke a supernatural sanction for their maxims and to go forth and preach them to the whole world? I am at a loss to reply; because I can find little in their recommendations except a cautious allegiance to the genteel tradition. But can the way of Matthew Arnold and of Professor Norton be the way of life for all men for ever? If there be really a single supernatural vocation latent in all souls, I can imagine it revealed to some supreme sage in a tremendous vision, like that which came to Buddha under the Bo-Tree, or to Socrates when he heard, or dreamt that he heard, the Sibyl of Mantinaea discoursing on mortal and immortal love. There is much in any man's experience, if he reflects, to persuade him that the circumstances of this life are a strange accident to him, and that he belongs by nature to a different world. If all the American humanists had become Catholics like Newman, or even like Mr. T. S. Eliot, I should understand the reason.

But can it be that all Latins and Slavs, all Arabs, Chinamen, and Indians, if they were not benighted in mind and degenerate in body, would be model Anglo-Americans? That is what British and American politicians and missionaries seem to believe: all nations are expected gladly to exchange their religion and their customs for the protestant genteel tradition. I am myself an ardent admirer of the Anglo-American character. I almost share that "extraordinary faith in the moral efficacy of cold baths and dumb-bells" which Mr. Bertrand Russell attributes to the Y.M.C.A. Sport, companionship, reading-rooms, with an occasional whiff of religious sentiment to stop foul mouths and turn aside hard questions —all this composes a saving tonic for the simple masculine soul habitually in the service of Big Business; while for the more fastidious, or the more fashionable, I can see the value of the English public school and the Anglican Church, which Mr. Russell thinks mere instruments of oppression. To me—seeing them, I confess, at a more romantic distance —they seem instruments rather of a beautiful integration: none of those fierce darts of intellectual sincerity which Mr. Russell would like, but something voluminous, comfortable, and sane, on a political, conventional, and sporting level.

The senses, which we use successfully in action, distort the objects on which we act, yet do so harmlessly and poetically, because our bodies are quick to understand those perceptions before our minds have had time to consider them narrowly. In the same way understanding relieves a truly intelligent man from fussiness about social institutions and conventions: they are absurd, yet absurdity is not incompatible with their natural function, which may be indispensable. But in philosophy, when ultimately the spirit comes face to face with the truth, convention and absurdity are out of place; so is humanism and so is the genteel tradition; so is morality itself.

The commandment *Thou shalt not kill,* for instance, is given out on divine authority, and infinite sanctions are supposed to confirm it in the other world. Yet the basis of this commandment is not cosmic or supernatural, but narrowly human. It expresses the natural affection of kindred for one another, an affection surviving and woefully rebuking any rash murder; and it expresses also the social and political need of living, within a certain territory, in safety and mutual trust. In its human atmosphere, the thunder of that precept is therefore not hollow; the sharp bolts of remorse and ruin follow closely upon it. But in the cosmos at large, is killing forbidden? If so, the fabric of creation must be monstrous and sinful indeed. The moving equilibrium of things, so blind and inexorable, yet often so magnificent, becomes a riddle to be deciphered, a labyrinth of punishments and favors, the work of some devil, or at least a work of God so contaminated with evil as to be a caricature of the divine intentions. And not in human life only: the ferocity and agony of the jungle and the strange gropings of life in the depths of the sea, become perverse and scandalous; existence seems a disease, and the world a garden of poisons, through which a man must pick his way with fear and trembling, girded high, and dreading to touch the earth with his bare foot, or a fellow-creature with his hand. Had it been the Creator who said *Thou shalt not kill,* and said it to the universe, existence would have been arrested.

When therefore a tender conscience extends its maxims beyond their natural basis, it not only ceases to be rational in its deliverances, and becomes fanatical, but it casts the livid colors of its own insanity upon nature at large. A strained holiness, never without its seamy side, ousts honorable virtue, and the fear of so many enemies becomes the greatest enemy of the soul. No true appreciation of anything is possible without a sense of its *naturalness*, of the innocent necessity by which it has assumed its special and perhaps extraordinary form. In a word, the principle of morality is naturalistic. Call it humanism or not, only a morality frankly relative to man's nature is worthy of man, being at once vital and rational, martial and generous; whereas absolutism smells of fustiness as well as of faggots.

Index

Index

Printed in the United States
131196LV00001B/169-183/A